KING
CHARLES III

KING CHARLES III

40 Years of Architecture

CLIVE ASLET

TRIGLYPH
BOOKS

First published in the United Kingdom in 2025 by Triglyph Books.

Triglyph Books
154 Tachbrook Street
London SW1V 2NE
www.triglyphbooks.com

Instagram: @triglyphbooks

Publisher: Clive Aslet and Dylan Thomas
Production Manager: Kate Turner
Typesetting: Palimpsest Book Production Ltd
Series design concept: Tetragon, London
Series cover design concept: Ocky Murray
Assistant Editor: Devon Harvey
Research Assistant: Rebecca Lilley
Copyeditor: Henry Howard
Proofreader: Mike Turner

British Library Cataloguing-in-Publication Data.
A catalogue record for this book is available from the British Library.

ISBN: 978-1-7397314-5-8 (hardback)
ISBN: 978-1-0686914-0-9 (ebook)
ISBN: 978-1-0686914-1-6 (audiobook)

Printed and bound sustainably in China.

To Dylan

'Architecture has its political Use; publick Buildings being the Ornament of a Country; it establishes a Nation, draws People and Commerce; makes the People love their native Country, which Passion is the Original of all great Actions in a Common-wealth.'

SIR CHRISTOPHER WREN,
TRACT I ON ARCHITECTURE

'Perhaps they will appreciate the things I try to do after I am dead ... !'

LETTER FROM H.R.H. PRINCE CHARLES
THE PRINCE OF WALES TO DUDLEY
POPLAK, DECEMBER 11, 1992.[1]

Contents

Acknowledgements

I HAVE SPOKEN TO MANY PEOPLE IN THE WRITING OF this book, not all of whom have wanted to be credited in the body of the text. I am grateful to all of them, however shy. A number of those who helped also read the text, in whole or in part. Special thanks in this respect go to Julian and Isabel Bannerman, Andrew Hamilton, Brian Hanson, James Knox, Jules Lubbock, Ben Pentreath, Hugh Petter, Alireza Sagharchi, Charles Saumarez Smith and John Simpson. Some of my visits and discussions have taken place over years, if not decades, although the book itself is a recent project. So some of the above have had a lot of me to put up with. Needless to say, Léon Krier has had a central role and every conversation with him has been a delight. In addition I must thank Sophie Andreae, Alan Baxter, Ben Bolgar, Dan Cruickshank, Alastair Dick-Cleland, Philip Fry, Catherine Goodman, Mark Hoare, Peter Lacey, Christopher Martin, Charles Morris, Paul Murrain, Liam O'Connor, Alan Powers, Richard Sammons, George Saumarez Smith, Ross Sharpe, James Stourton, Sir Roy Strong, Quinlan Terry, Joanna Wachowiak and Kim Wilkie. Rebecca Lilley has shared the research burden and magically kept the project on track. My wonderful colleagues at Triglyph Books – Kate Turner, India Brooker and Devon Harvey – have spread joy at every turn. Dylan Thomas, my partner in Triglyph, kept me up to the mark, as well as taking some of the photographs. Sons William, Johnny and Charlie provided an invaluable sounding board, as did my wife Naomi: I particularly value her response to Poundbury when we stayed at the Duchess of Cornwall Inn.

This is not an authorised book and I had no access to His Majesty King Charles III while writing it, but over the course of my career I have been lucky enough to follow him around the Duchy of Cornwall as well as meeting him on a few other occasions. I would like to say, somewhat after the event, how grateful I am for the glimpses they afforded into his great passion for buildings and building. One day, the subject of King Charles III and Architecture will be addressed by scholars of the future, who will find a treasure trove of memos, letters and annotated plans in the Royal Archive. This cannot be claimed of my book. Instead I have the advantage of writing from first-hand accounts from many of the key players, still happily alive, and my own observations from the ring-side seat I have occupied over the years.

Introduction

VERYONE KNOWS THAT KING CHARLES III IS BIG on architecture. It is one of the great royal enthusiasms, along with the armed forces, organic farming, homoeopathy, wildflower meadows, the King James Bible and warning the world about climate change. But the extent of his involvement in architecture has never been fully presented to the public. When HM was HRH The Prince of Wales, the media had other narratives. They wanted stories about Princess Diana, Camilla, his supposed frustration at biding his time for the throne, his 'black spider' memos to government ministers, his extravagance, the contrast between his privilege and the lives of most of his subjects. The hope he gave to a destitute former mining community in East Ayrshire by reviving Dumfries House with a host of training opportunities was largely ignored. Local enthusiasm for the Prince's initiatives, such as Dumfries House, rarely gave rise to positive headlines in the national media. A journalist I know accepted a commission to write a belittling newspaper piece about Poundbury, the Prince of Wales's model extension to Dorchester; he thought he knew it but at the time had not actually been there. Afterwards, he visited and found much to admire. Even I was surprised by the charm of the place when I returned for this book, despite several previous visits. When I first went, it had just been built and therefore looked new and raw. The streets have now mellowed to the point that many people will soon think they have always been there. Dumfries House and Poundbury are but two examples of Charles's public engagement with architecture during his time as Prince of Wales, most of which has been uncelebrated, misunderstood or forgotten.

My aim is to draw together many different aspects of the King's interest in architecture since he made his 'carbuncle' speech to the potentates of the Royal Institute of British Architects in 1984. That was 40 years ago. The carbuncle itself – an unsympathetic addition to the National Gallery – was overcome and replaced by a more elegant building. Similarly, a Modernist proposal to crowd the precincts of St Paul's with aggressive office buildings was quashed, its place taken by a more humane scheme instigated by the Prince. Controversy continued into the 21st century, when Richard Rogers's proposal for a gated development on the Chelsea Barracks site was withdrawn by its investors, a branch of the Qatari sovereign wealth fund, after a word 'Prince to Prince'. 'This sort of situation is totally unconstitutional,' raged Rogers, and perhaps he had a point. But the replacement by Squire and Partners, Dixon Jones and Kim Wilkie Associates has the benefit that Londoners are not exiled from this part of the city but can enjoy the public spaces and planting it offers: they could only have seen the Rogers development from behind railings.

In the early days, the Prince supported Community Architecture, based on the novel idea that the tenants who would be the end users of new housing estates should be asked their views on the sort of accommodation they would like to live in before their new homes were built. By the time of Paternoster Square, his focus had turned to Classicism. Only a tiny band of diehards had managed to keep the Classical flame alive since the Second World War; they were the underdogs and deserved a champion, since Classicism is as valid a style for the modern age as any other. I can confirm, from personal conversation when he was Prince, that the King loves Classicism, but it must be said at the outset that he loves many other things too. He is one of the few people alive who reads the Victorian sage John Ruskin. This alone would suggest that his natural sympathies are with the Arts and Crafts Movement. That the sacred geometry of Islamic pattern unites the universe (and can be expressed in architecture) is an article of faith for him. He also has a very English taste for whimsy, found in the local curiosities and the homespun nature of traditional architecture, as well as in the many old and singular buildings that he helped save through the Phoenix Trust. These included enormous Victorian textile mills whose scale made them appear an eccentric object of affection in the late 20th century; converted to apartments and shopping complexes, they are now

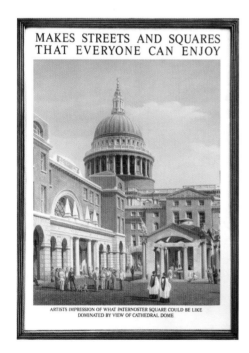

MAKES STREETS AND SQUARES
THAT EVERYONE CAN ENJOY

ARTISTS IMPRESSION OF WHAT PATERNOSTER SQUARE COULD BE LIKE
DOMINATED BY VIEW OF CATHEDRAL DOME

Poster from 1987 showing John Simpson's vision for Paternoster Square, next to St Paul's Cathedral in the City of London. The principle of making streets and squares that everyone can enjoy was fully endorsed by Prince Charles.

so prosperous and attractive that it is hardly possible to remember that they were once slated for demolition. Whimsy is the stuff of Charles's garden at Highgrove House in the Cotswolds. You can visit the garden: it is open to anyone who buys a ticket. There you will see all these aspects of his personality expressed in an intensely personal Arcadia, part of which, until he gave up the lease, was a pioneering organic farm.

A different kind of Arcadia exists in rural Romania, parts of which, due to the inefficiency and backwardness of the old Communist regime, did not suffer the destructive effects of industrial agriculture or commercial development in the second half of the 20th century. By owning two homes in Transylvania, the King shows that the area had something precious – its unspoilt beauty – which the rest of the world would pay to come and see. This could provide a better means of improving the economy than conventional growth strategies, which would destroy local diversity and repeat mistakes now being rued by other countries. As Charles told a meeting of American architects in 1990,

> we don't have to keep on rushing headlong into the 'future' as if the whole of history were a hundred-yard dash. As Mahatma Gandhi said 'There is more to life than going faster'. We can permit ourselves to move 'inward' – into tradition – 'outward' – into Nature – and 'upward' – to the heavens – along the way.

Perhaps to their bafflement, he quoted from T.S. Eliot's *Four Quartets* to prove it.

The Duchy of Cornwall has followed Poundbury with other schemes, notably Nansledan outside Newquay and a proposal for Faversham. They have been ahead of their time in their thinking about walkable neighbourhoods, sustainability and localism. In the decade from 1991, Charles's team ran summer schools and a school for architecture and the crafts, under the aegis of the Prince of Wales's Institute of Architecture, the forerunner of the King's Foundation; they were schools like no other, often chaotic, but capable of attracting a galaxy of stars in their field to stimulate and inspire the students. Many of the students found the experience life changing. All this has taken place in Britain, in the teeth of a hostile press and quite often against the wishes of palace officials, who have had other priorities to pursue (such as ensuring the Prince would marry again and become King – objectives that, to be fair, have been successfully accomplished). Architects and powers around the world have also noticed what the Prince was up to. One senior diplomat from the Middle East says that the King has done more to support the cause of Islamic art than any of the crown princes of his own region.

Thus the King's 40 years of architecture as Prince of Wales is a big topic with many threads. Some of those close to His Majesty would say that it is not a discrete subject but part of a larger whole that embraces all the King's interests, which share the one goal of reuniting mankind with the ancient Harmony of the world, which has been blown apart by the Industrial Revolution, globalisation and human greed. (I capitalise Harmony because it is key to the royal vision.) But architecture, in my view, deserves its own book, not least because the King's achievement has never been fully recognised; nor has it been taken as seriously as it should. Indeed, it has often been pilloried. Attitudes, however, may be changing, making this an appropriate moment for the book. At the time of the Coronation, there was a general taking stock of the man who was the new head of state. Having spent decades pooh-poohing much of his work and laughing at his ideas, the media found that he had often been right on the big things, making the correct judgement call years before the rest of the world had caught onto them. He was right on the environment and climate change. There is much to be said for organic farming, given the need to repair depleted soils, even if it does not provide a means of feeding a hungry world and may not be helpful in reducing greenhouse emissions; despite royal advocacy, the market share for organic food in the UK has barely changed in all the time that Prince Charles was farming organically, hovering around one per cent. But as the gardener Isabel Bannerman observes, 'ecological conservation and regeneration have moved from being cranky and odd to being received wisdom'. So has he been proved right on architecture? In many respects, yes.

Architecture was nothing that Britain could be proud of in the decades following the Second World War. Arguably it had begun to improve before the Prince's involvement – but only marginally; the standard of most commercial development, most volume house building and most of the new architecture on Britain's streets was below par. The Prince showed there was another way. Poundbury and Nansledan demonstrate that it is possible to create communities where affordable and open-market homes exist side by side and nobody knows the difference; where the car takes second place, small shops and businesses can flourish and everything needed to support life and work is within walking distance. Architecture does not have to be monolithic, as it was in the 1970s, subject to a single ideology whose virtue was understood only by members of the profession; a thousand flowers can bloom. The ideal of Harmony has not been widely publicised, but most people would accept that humankind needs a closer rapport with Nature, for the wellbeing of the individual if nothing else. He has influenced taste by supporting a myriad of small causes across the land, sometimes identified during the course of incognito trips (perhaps taken in an Aston Martin driven with reckless disregard for the security detail attempting to keep up in the car behind) made with the gardeners Isabel and Julian Bannerman

This image from the cover of the *Illustrated London News*'s Royal issue in 1989 looks askance at some examples of recent architecture in the capital. Two years earlier Prince Charles had told an audience at the Mansion House that the Luftwaffe did not replace the buildings it destroyed 'with anything more offensive than rubble. We did that.'

or Sir John Betjeman's daughter Candida Lycett Green. His reach extends beyond these isles to the 40 countries in which INTBAU – a network of traditional architects around the world which the Prince founded in 2001, with Robert Adam as chair – has chapters. It is impossible to compute what his espousal of hand craftsmanship and traditional building materials has meant to INTBAU members in Pakistan, Malaysia, the Philippines and elsewhere, but architects who follow non-conformist paths know that they do not stand alone.

There is another reason for my writing this book. The period covered coincides with my career as a journalist, in which architecture and the countryside played a large role. I have therefore followed the story closely. Sometimes I literally followed the Prince, trailing in his wake as he toured the Duchy of Cornwall's estates in the West Country and the Scilly Isles – a nerve-wracking experience, since he moved at speed, often by helicopter, making it difficult to keep up; as the sole journalist present I would listen respectfully to his conversations with farmers about the charming effects of ringworm or anaerobic effluent digesters. (If my mind ever wandered, that would be the moment when he would say, 'I'd say this barn is 18th century. What do you think, Clive?' and I would have to wake up with a start.) Occasionally, at receptions, we exchanged words and what struck me most was his knowledge. After half a century of travelling the globe, speaking to endless numbers of people, meeting on one-to-one terms the greatest experts in any subject you would care to name, as well as being shown interminably around the factories, farms, housing estates, places of worship and community halls of his kingdom, the memory bank of his naturally enquiring mind is formidably well stocked. This may not make Charles uniquely wise but experience means that he often knows more on a given topic than even specialist journalists. And with knowledge goes passion; there could be no doubting – a few seconds speaking with him are enough to reveal it – that the Prince cared deeply about setting architecture on a better course and making the world a better place for people to live in.

He may be self-indulgent, prone to outbursts of temper, apt to jet around the planet while preaching the need to save it from climate change, impractical, bad at choosing staff, unfamiliar with

'A City Fit for a King': the mysterious Featherbottom & Partners reimagine some prominent London landmarks in tongue-in-cheek homage to Charles III's taste for architectural variety and caprice. To quote their website, 'We favour traditional and classical design in line with the Kings' [*sic*] architectural critique, inspired from his teachings and examples to create a more beautiful Britain to his liking.'

the principles on which businesses are managed – but if so, the failings are part of a complex and fascinating individual. Critics who say that his opinion on the nationally important subject of architecture is of no more value than anyone else's are surely wide of the mark. He has spent a lifetime thinking about it and informing himself. Having the courage of his convictions, he used his estate, the Duchy of Cornwall, to experiment, putting into practice the ideas and beliefs he has honed. In the main they have been more successful than he could ever have hoped and have stimulated a revolution in UK planning. For this depth of experience he should if anything be regarded – apart from the role he plays as head of state – as a great national resource. Architecture is not a party-political subject, by and large. It is a thousand pities that by ascending the throne King Charles III's lips have been sealed on a subject he cares so much about.

ONE

CARBUNCLE

The Hampton Court Speech and The National Gallery

On May 30, 1984, the miners' leader Arthur Scargill was arrested outside a South Yorkshire coking works during the long-running miners' strike; the television travel journalist Alan Whicker was photographed using the first machine capable of issuing rail tickets automatically at Euston Station; and the Royal Institute of British Architects was holding a Festival of Architecture to coincide with its 150th anniversary. That evening it would throw a gala dinner at Hampton Court Palace.

Architects had been busy since the Second World War with the massive programmes of rebuilding mounted both by government and developers. Swathes of Britain's cities, their terraces run down through lack of investment and pockmarked with bomb sites, had been demolished and replaced with blocks of flats. High-rise hotels and office buildings sprang up to evoke the glamour of American commerce, at a time when the New World shone much brighter than the Old. Developers told the councillors of Kettering, Bognor Regis and many, many other towns they had to keep pace with the times. Friendly streets and proud civic

The Prince of Wales leaves the podium after delivering the 'carbuncle' speech at Hampton Court in 1984. Having just presented the RIBA gold medal to the Indian architect Charles Correa, he wears a flower garland around his neck – a festive touch at odds with the mood his words had engendered.

traditions were not enough to stay abreast of the modern world; unless they demolished a large area of urban fabric and built supermarkets, shopping centres and municipal office blocks, surrounded by a sea of tarmac, they would fall behind. 'For the use of the people, for the good of the city,' read a translation of the RIBA's Latin motto, coined in the 1830s. But the recent President of the RIBA Owen Luder gave the game away when he said admiringly of Richard Rogers's 1982 competition entry for an extension to the National Gallery in Trafalgar Square:

> That is the work of a man who has said, 'That is what I think the answer is, and sod you.'

Architecture is the most public of the arts; its impact on those who live nearby, walk past it every day or work inside it is inescapable. You might have thought that ordinary people were entitled to a view on it. But Luder was a Brutalist. He and other senior members of the profession raised two fingers to the public who would be living, sometimes literally, in the shadow of their work. After their long training, architects were like doctors and other professional people of the day: they saw themselves as something of a priestly caste to whom the sacred mysteries had been revealed on an exclusive basis. Opinions expressed by a population uneducated in such matters were of little interest.

The sun shone and the ancient brick palace of Hampton Court looked its best. In black tie or, being who they were, polo necks, members disappeared into the State Rooms for a drink before emerging to gather round a podium on one of the courtyard lawns. Most did so with high hearts. They were to be addressed by the Prince of Wales. It was traditional for members of the Royal Family to be wheeled out on professional occasions such as this – they added tone, stamped them with a royal seal of approval. The RIBA had done well to get the heir to the throne, who was younger and perceived as more exciting than his parents, particularly since his marriage to Princess Diana in 1981. But mutterings of anxiety could be heard in some quarters. Earlier that day, the President and Council of the RIBA had been sent a copy of the speech he would deliver. A version had also been given to *The Times*, which would print it at the head of its op-ed page the next day.

The constitution requires the Royal Family to eschew politics. By convention they avoid controversy. Since the nearly disastrous episode of Edward VIII's abdication, his successors – George VI and Elizabeth II – had put on a mask of dullness to the public, avoiding any subject that could have ruffled feathers. Most people had little idea of HM The Queen's private opinions about anything, although she certainly had them. Admittedly, her husband the Duke of Edinburgh would become famous, as the century wore on and the media became less respectful, for gaffes about 'ghastly' Stoke-on-Trent – amongst other remarks. But these reflected the natural off-the-cuff exuberance and, at times, frustration of a salty character. His formal speeches could be outspoken but steered clear of giving offence. Royal observers should perhaps have spotted that the Prince of Wales would set a different tone. Now in his mid-30s, he had begun to strike an intellectual note in his speeches, at odds with the caricature philistinism of the upper classes. On being given an honorary degree at Oxford in 1983, he spoke of 'perception' as:

> the sort of quality which can lead towards the creation of an all-important balance between the world within and the world without; between material things and eternal things; between orthodox and unorthodox; between science and religion.

He then quoted from the psychiatrist Carl Jung, whose works he is supposed to have read on his honeymoon with Princess Diana; Jung believed that human beings were linked by a collective unconscious informed by deep instincts to which they had access at birth.

In time, the need to rediscover balance or Harmony in the world became a major, indeed all-encompassing, theme for the Prince of Wales. Since 1970 he had been sounding off about the environment and had begun to mention alternative medicine. But in his many public engagements, he had run true to royal form. There had been no frightening of the horses. Most of Charles's audience at Hampton Court expected their egos to be stroked.

And with reason. Boldly, they had chosen to give that year's gold medal to the Indian architect Charles Correa, a man of great eloquence and charm, married to an artist-weaver: his career had been dedicated to improving living conditions in poor and chaotic cities such as Mumbai. For Correa and India, which had already honoured this humanitarian, it was a great moment, and Correa ought surely to have appealed to HRH. But the top brass had discovered that Prince Charles would not tickle their corporate tummy. In fact his tone would be abrasive. Hampton Court ceased to evoke the jollity of vast Henrician feasts so much as that royal tyrant's propensity for chopping off people's heads.

Blade thin from his love of adrenalin-fuelled sports, the Prince rose and walked to the microphone, a two-inch scar from a kick during a polo match at Windsor four years earlier still livid on his cheek. No doubt he fingered his shirt cuffs or twisted his signet ring as he usually did, a displacement activity that quelled nerves. It had been a difficult speech to write. He had agonised over it and had only finished the final draft that morning. But he briefly smiled as he removed the folded sheets of typescript from his pocket. One imagines that the President and Council's blood ran cold.

The speech opened with a salute to Correa. This paragraph would later be criticised as too brief; at any rate it was overshadowed by the explosive content that would come later. From Correa, Charles moved to Prince Albert, the Prince Consort, his great-great-great grandfather, whom he described as a kind of architectural hypochondriac – someone for whom the love of building was almost a neurosis. This may have amused his audience, as the Prince intended – the remoteness of the Victorian age made it difficult to take seriously. Few could have appreciated, though, that the Prince himself considered his forebear an admirable role model who combined the highest standards of public service with a determination to face down vested interests; a royal personage with decided opinions of his own. But alarm bells began to clang when Charles referred, with approval, to the 'reaction [against] the Modern Movement, which seems to be taking place in our society'. To many of those present, the Modern Movement was not so much a style in architecture as revealed truth. They had not abandoned the doctrine of the founding fathers, which prescribed it as the only logical, efficient and moral way to create buildings in the 20th century, the age of reinforced concrete and plate glass. Ornament was degenerate, all historical references (other than those made to the works of Le Corbusier, Mies van der Rohe and Walter Gropius) dismissed as worthless pastiche.

In truth, Modernism's game was already up and had been ever since a 22-storey tower block in East London called Ronan Point had partially collapsed following a gas explosion in 1968. The structural principles were fallible. High-rise council blocks, already so unpopular with tenants moved from old terraced streets, were not only alienating but unsafe. Then, in 1977, a slim polemical book by David Watkin entitled *Morality and Architecture* knocked away the intellectual props of Modernism's tottering edifice. 'The architectural profession and its commentators were outraged at this blasphemy,' wrote professor Alan Powers in the *Guardian*'s obituary of Watkin.[1] The King had almost certainly read Watkin's book, since the author was one of a small group who advised him in July 1987 as he considered what could be done about Paternoster Square, next to St Paul's.

Already some famous architects – and former Modernists – had turned away from the joyless puritanism of the Modern Movement and begun to flirt with ornament. On Madison Avenue in New York, Philip Johnson saucily added a Chippendale-like pediment to the top of his AT&T, in a calculated act of apostasy. But Johnson was reviled by the true believers. The old faith died hard.

Not surprisingly, given his upbringing, Charles liked old buildings. A romantic, the warp and weft of traditional streets spoke to him. He naturally gravitated to towns whose fabric had evolved over time. Ornate façades, old-fashioned materials and the human scale appealed to him. In this his taste was hardly radical, but equally it was regarded with some embarrassment by the intellectual elite. The annals of SAVE Britain's Heritage show how little sway it had among planners (whose prejudices were sometimes more extreme than those of architects; like academics, they did not have to sell their ideas to clients.) But hope for a better future was dawning. As the Prince told the assembled members of the RIBA,

> At last, after witnessing the wholesale destruction of Georgian and Victorian housing in most of our cities, people have begun to realise that it is possible to restore old buildings and what is more, that there are architects willing to undertake such projects.

There were, but few had been educated to do so. Except for interior design courses, architecture students received no training in conservation. Their mantra of 'tear down and rebuild' led 'a large number of us [to] have developed a feeling that architects tend to design houses for the approval of fellow architects and critics, not for the tenants'. Still, he was able to name two architects of whom he approved, one being Rod Hackney who went on to become President of the RIBA itself in 1987–9. The other was Ted Cullinan, described as being 'a man after my own heart, as he believes strongly that the architect must produce something that is visually beautiful as well as socially useful'. Both Hackney and Cullinan practised Community Architecture, thought of as being a walk on the wild side. The idea was that the end users of the buildings being designed should be consulted with the object of meeting their needs, spatial preferences and aesthetic desire; it was revolutionary at the time.

It was towards the end of the speech that the Prince fired the equivalent of two Exocets, the missiles recently in deadly use during the Falklands War. The first was to shoot down an eccentric proposal by the property developer Peter Palumbo to build a high-rise tower by Mies van der Rohe on Mansion House Square, near St Paul's Cathedral. Lord Palumbo, as he would become in Margaret Thatcher's resignation honours list, was a property developer – on the whole a dirty word at the time when skulduggery in that area of business was rife: the Labour Chancellor Denis Healey had sought to 'squeeze' property speculators 'until the pips squeak'. But he was also a collector and man of taste, as well as, coincidentally, a polo-playing companion of the Prince. A firm believer in the genius of Mies, he had commissioned him to design the tower in the 1960s, in the belief that it would bring the work of a world-renowned architect to London, whose post-war architecture had been mediocre. But Mies had died in 1969. Palumbo was therefore championing a building designed over a decade and a half earlier by an architect who could no longer supervise its construction. 'God is in the details,' Mies had famously said. Here it would now be left to God, rather than the architect, to get them right. The Prince's dismissal of the project as 'yet another giant glass stump, better suited to downtown Chicago than the City of London,' doomed its chances – already uncertain – of being given planning permission. One–love to the Prince.

'Glass stump' entered the language as a popular shorthand for skyscraper. 'Carbuncle on the face of a much-loved and elegant friend', the sobriquet he applied to the extension to the National Gallery in Trafalgar Square that had been subject to a public inquiry, also became a household phrase. It was brilliantly chosen and launched Charles on a new trajectory: using the voice given to him by his position, he would speak truth to a profession that he regarded as pompous and insensitive to public opinion. The National Gallery extension was a sitting duck. Few people could defend the building that had come into his sights, although its faults were as much those of a system – the way that government procured buildings – as of the architects whom Charles singled out.

The history of the scheme illustrates the British establishment's measly attitude towards architecture at the time of the Prince's intervention. Official parsimony had deep roots, as the last Charles on the throne – Charles II – would have confirmed: he was never able to build the new palace he had wanted. Absolutist monarchs on the other side of the English Channel had more resources to command than the crowned head of a constitutional monarchy,

Model of Ahrends, Burton and Koralek's proposal for the National Gallery extension, Trafalgar Square: famously condemned by Prince Charles in 1984 as 'a monstrous carbuncle on the face of a much-loved and elegant friend'.

answerable to Parliament. While 20th-century French presidents continued to take pride in the spectacular additions they made to Paris – the *grands projets* that often bear their name – few British prime ministers since Sir Robert Walpole have taken much interest in the visual arts. By tradition, competitions for great government buildings were dogged by meanness, compromise and delay. The National Gallery competition ran true to form. A malign combination of political ego and dogmatic penny-pinching made a sow's ear of it. Nobody could have made the result into a silk purse. It was an impossible challenge which put the winners Ahrends, Burton and Koralek (ABK) in the firing line, unfairly it could be said – but then they did not have to take the job.

The story opens in 1980, when the new chairman of the trustees of the National Gallery, Lord Annan, discovered that the director, Michael Levey, urgently needed more space. Unfortunately, the auguries for getting it were particularly unpropitious, since the Thatcher government was determined to bear down on inflation by controlling public expenditure of all kinds. Even so, the trustees pressed ahead, proposing that an old warehouse which had been acquired for the use of the gallery in 1958 should be demolished to provide the site of an extension. This was done less in the hope that the Department of the Environment would agree to the project – other museums and galleries had already been turned down – than that the trustees would not be required to sell the land: government departments had been instructed to dispose of surplus landholdings in the name of efficiency. As expected, the money for the extension was not forthcoming. Then, as he later recalled in a lecture, Annan

> floated an idea. The Museum of Modern Art and the Whitney Museum in New York had both sold their site to developers

and had obtained new premises financed by the commercial development above them. Could we do the same?

In the case of the National Gallery, the galleries would have been on the top floor of the extension, to connect with the main floor of the National Gallery itself, with commercial offices below.

When the suggestion was put to the Secretary of State for the Environment, Michael Heseltine,

> he fell about with delight. It was exactly the kind of partnership between the private and public sector that the government wanted to encourage. At minimal cost to the tax-payer the State would get an extension to the second most important of the national collections.

Heseltine's enthusiasm was to prove a mixed blessing. He took over the scheme and appointed Sir Hugh Casson, President of the Royal Academy, to oversee the competition to choose an architect. Annan and Levey, whose brief specified 'rather church or basilica-like' spaces appropriate to the early Renaissance pictures which the extension would house, were side-lined. Casson wanted to allow the competing architects maximum freedom of invention; incredibly, the competitors were not allowed to speak to any employee of the National Gallery. The winners, ABK, were not Annan and Levey's favoured team: they would have preferred the American firm of Skidmore, Owings and Merrill. Commercial pressures meant that the office element of the scheme expanded at the expense of the galleries. The scene was set for an architectural disaster. A carbuncle was almost bound to result.

It may have been unkind of the Prince to blame ABK for their scheme without mentioning the conflicting priorities and behind-the-scenes wrangling which had been midwife to the ill-featured baby. The harsh spotlight he shone on them almost destroyed the practice. On the other hand, their design was awful; although only an adjunct to the reticent Neo-Classicism of William Wilkins's National Gallery of 1832 – less appreciated then than now – it called attention to itself in a glaring and fussy way. The materials and form were alien to the existing building. A spiky glazed tower poked above the whole as a counterbalance to the spire of St Martin-in-the-Fields. It was pasted by the critics. And yet only one of them was prepared to lodge an official objection with the public inquiry into the project instituted by Heseltine's successor as secretary of state, which would have meant a hostile cross-examination by highly paid barristers. The exception was the *Observer's* Stephen Gardiner who believed, idealistically, that commerce should not be allowed to taint high art. He did not criticise the form or materials of the architecture itself. 'A striking feature of the enquiry was the lack of involvement and attendance,' said the inspector who ran it. If critics in the fourth estate and arts establishment had engaged more fully with what they saw as the enemy, it might not have been so necessary for the Prince of Wales to fire off his broadside. When he did so, it would be devastating:

Instead of designing an extension to the elegant façade of the National Gallery which complements it and continues the concept of columns and domes, it looks as if we may be presented with a kind of municipal fire station, complete with the sort of tower that contains the siren ... what is proposed is like a monstrous carbuncle on the face of a much-loved and elegant friend. Apart from anything else it defeats me why anyone wishing to display the early Renaissance pictures belonging to the Gallery should do so in a new gallery so manifestly at odds with the whole spirit of that age of astonishing proportion.

The ABK scheme was holed below the waterline. Nigel Broackes of the developer Trafalgar House told Peter Ahrends as much the next day. 'We were all very shocked at the nature of the intervention,' recalled Ahrends. Later, the Prince had attempted a reconciliation with the practice by inviting Peter Ahrends to a dinner at Kensington Palace, where he sat next to the Prince, and visiting their offices. After viewing their work with apparent approval, he said 'I'm sorry it had to be you.' To which another partner, Richard Burton replied, 'Not half as sorry as we were!'(A version of the story has it that the practice replied: 'We're sorry it had to be you.' Which sounds as if it was polished after the event.)

There was, except for ABK, a happy ending to the debacle. Lord Sainsbury came forward, convincing his brothers and Lord Rothschild, the National Gallery's chairman of trustees, that they should jointly sponsor the extension, thereafter to be known as the Sainsbury Wing. The winners of the new competition were the American Post-Modernists Robert Venturi and Denise Scott Brown. Dry purists may criticise the snaking façade and somewhat random application of Classical orders as deviations from the strict Classical tradition, but the material of Portland stone and the fine Roman lettering were both in keeping. According to a later director, Charles Saumarez Smith, 'there can be no dispute that' the architects 'succeeded brilliantly' in providing 'a sympathetic environment for the early Italian collection',[2] exactly in the 'church or basilica-like' manner of the National Gallery's original brief. The broad internal staircase leading up to galleries is a masterpiece whose pleasure never palls for those using it.

Speaking after the Prince, Correa said he now knew what he would talk to him about at dinner. Flower garlands were then placed around both their necks and they left the podium in festive guise. Looks were deceptive. There were so many people at the dinner that it was served in numerous rooms, in two sittings. The Prince's table consisted of Correa and a select number of RIBA bigwigs. According to the Prince's biographer Jonathan Dimbleby, it ended in 'an atmosphere suffused with repressed anger', with the hosts longing for Charles to leave.

A counterattack from the profession was inevitable. 'Modern architecture is in danger of being obliterated by an indiscriminate wave of nostalgia,' fulminated Richard Rogers, later Baron Rogers of Riverside, in a letter to *The Times*. How absurd to think that the public disliked modern architecture when so many visitors mobbed the Centre Beaubourg in Paris, which he had designed with Renzo Piano. Progressive buildings, so often pilloried by ignorant contemporaries when they went up, become tomorrow's masterpieces, widely loved and admired. What need had such works to conform to the urban context in which they stood? They transcended humdrum considerations of space and time.

> … great art of different periods has a common language which bridges time.

> A better understanding of history is essential, but uninformed criticism and the romanticising of the past are not the ways to build a better environment for today.

An Anglo-Italian, Rogers understood about vendettas and the one he launched against the Prince in 1984 lasted until his death in 2021.

'Modern architecture is not dead,' wrote Michael Manser. 'There always has been modern architecture and there always will be modern architecture.' Never had British architecture, he continued in a side-swipe at the Prince, been more democratic, given that it was controlled either by the planning system or the elected

Corinthian capitals on the Sainsbury Wing of the National Gallery, derived from the Arch of Hadrian in Athens, erected in 131 AD. The Post-Modernist licence with which Venturi, Scott Brown and Associates bunched classical elements together affronted classical purists but created a lively façade while paying tribute to the style of the main building.

Venturi, Scott Brown's Sainsbury Wing of the National Gallery, 1991, shown in the context of the original building of the 1830s. The addition adopts the cornice line and materials of William Wilkins's masterpiece, while distributing pilasters at irregular intervals across the façade.

politicians who were ultimately responsible for the government, local government and government agency projects that had until recently accounted for half of all building in the country. The public just needed time to see the beauties of new and apparently alien structures which they had thought hideous at first sight.

> Our whole urban inheritance is one of contrasts of succeeding styles and no generation was more disregarding of previous periods than the Victorians'. Was the Foreign Office a sympathetic companion to the little houses in Downing Street? Or Big Ben an appropriate neighbour to medieval Westminster Hall?

In the heat of battle, Manser had failed to notice that Big Ben was not a good example to make the point, given that it is covered in tracery and sculpture that is medieval in inspiration. But he had other carbuncular edifices, now happily accepted, up his sleeve.

> More recently, in the 1930s, was Peter Jones's store in scale to Sloane Square? A very Mies van der Rohe type of conception. Or Simpson's [now Waterstones] appropriate to Piccadilly? Yet most of these contrasts are enjoyed and admired now.

The quotation is taken from an article by Manser which appeared in the *Sunday Times* on June 10, 1984. Nine days earlier he had been quoted by *The Times*'s architecture correspondent Charles Knevitt as saying: 'Wouldn't it be marvellous if the Duchy of Cornwall commissioned a modern building?' The Prince, he implied, could set a better architectural example through patronage than speech-making. Watch this space.

On the other side of Trafalgar Square, the Prince feared for the future of the Grand Hotel of 1880, which had been saved from demolition a decade earlier following a campaign. The international competition for its replacement attracted many futuristic proposals to celebrate, as Zaha Hadid Architects puts it, the 'dynamic possibilities of the urban landscape'. Conscious that anything too wild might attract a royal zinger, which would extend the planning process and cost money, the developers chose a scheme by Sidell Gibson Partnership, which hid an up-to-the-minute building with an atrium behind a façade that was almost indistinguishable from the old one. Fine words butter no parsnips, went the old saying. But when spoken by the Prince of Wales, they could. Across Britain façadism – retaining old façades and constructing new edifices behind them – became rife. It was hated by Modernists for its supposed lack of honesty, and by conservationists for preserving too few of the old rooms. But it preserved the proportions and friendliness of streets that would have otherwise been destroyed, not least in the City of London.

While Charles infuriated many architects, we have seen that he had other bases of support. The glass stump was not built, the carbuncle superseded by a better design. The advent of Post-Modernism showed that the world was changing. Generally the media divided on party lines: journalists who disliked the monarchy lamented his intervention, while royalists and right-wingers tended to support him. Few on either side could have predicted what would come next. More speeches, more outspokenness, a television programme, followed by interventions in the architectural debate that went beyond mere words. Speech-making, he told an audience of architects in 1987, provided 'one of my rare opportunities to stir things up, to throw a proverbial royal brick through the inviting plate glass of pompous, professional pride'. In that aim he was successful. At the time, even the Prince may not have known that the Hampton Court speech would not prove to be an isolated pot-shot at a captive audience so much as the opening salvo in an engagement that would last until his accession to the throne nearly 40 years later and – who knows? – may yet cause the odd explosion after that. Architecture would not prove to be a princely caprice so much as a lifelong passion.

Where did his ideas come from? Prince Charles had been a sensitive, cello-playing child, who was bullied by his peers at Gordonstoun; the Action Man image, as a fearless off-piste skier who took his many falls on the polo ground and hunting field without complaint, came later. The school art room had been a refuge. During the Baroque age and the Enlightenment, architecture had formed part of a princely education: monarchs had many uses for it, from fortification to palace-building. As a boy, George III had received lessons from Sir William Chambers. This tradition had lapsed by the 20th century. But Prince Charles's home background was hardly a visual desert. As well as growing up among splendid homes and amid works of art, he inherited a love of watercolour painting from his father the Duke of Edinburgh, who was also a keen amateur photographer.

Prince Philip championed modern industrial design in the 1950s and 1960s, urging firms whose product range still reflected the heavy values of the imperial past to match the aesthetic standards of their Continental and American competitors, whether or not they could meet the price point of the Japanese. This interest was spurred by the light, fresh, Scandinavian-influenced Festival of Britain of 1951, with its mission to brighten the spirits and living rooms of a nation still depressed by post-Second World War austerity; as well as the need to decorate the new *Royal Yacht Britannia*, on which the Duke worked with Casson. In 1959, the Design Council launched The Duke of Edinburgh's Prize for Elegant Design, later renamed The Prince Philip Designers Prize. The object was to improve the look and functionality of everyday things, the first winner being Charles Longman for his Prestcold

Packaway refrigerator, whose minimally adorned, rectangular lines were designed to fit into small kitchens. In this, Prince Philip was typical of his age, with its belief in the design solutions provided by engineering and dislike of clutter. Delighting in fancy and Classical richness, Prince Charles's taste was no less shaped by his era – that of Post-Modernism. Nevertheless, whatever the differences between father and son on this and other subjects, he grew up with a similar point of view to that of the Duke of Edinburgh: while personally enjoying architecture, decoration and gardening for their own sakes, he wanted to improve and elevate the conditions amid which ordinary people lived.

Unlike her husband, HM Queen Elizabeth II did not pronounce on matters of taste and only a few of her close friends can have known what she thought about them. That did not mean she did not have any. Domestically, her taste can be gauged from the comfortable chintziness of her bedroom on board *Britannia* – 'this is where I can truly relax,' she said of the royal yacht. It was unpretentious, homely and unchanging. Reluctant to spend money where it was not necessary to do so, and naturally conservative in her view of the monarchy, she kept Balmoral exactly as it had been in 'the Queen's' day – by which she meant Queen Victoria. On *Britannia* her bedlinen, embossed with the monogram 'HM the Queen', came from Queen Victoria's bedroom on a previous royal yacht. Had she liked modern architecture one might expect to find some trace of it around the estates and palaces that her family used. Instead the Modern Movement is conspicuous by its absence. Of course Her Majesty was better known as an expert rider, judge of horseflesh, trainer of gundogs, patroness of corgis and lover of the outdoors than as an aesthete. But she knew her way around the Royal Collection.

Queen Elizabeth the Queen Mother, to whom Prince Charles was close, bought modern British paintings (Augustus John,

One of a series of watercolours of Windsor Castle commissioned from John Piper by HM Queen Elizabeth the Queen Mother in 1942. Her taste influenced the young Prince Charles.

many Sickerts) and commissioned a series of 15 watercolours of Windsor Castle from John Piper – at £150, they were cheap at the price – and studies of horses. There were several clocks in each of her rooms, bespeaking an enthusiasm inherited by Charles and visible at Dumfries House. The result was not so much a collection as, in John Cornforth's words, 'an accumulation that has grown out of sheer pleasure in pictures and objects, and the enjoyment of the chase after them'. She 'always encouraged me to look and to observe,' the Prince wrote when dedicating his book *A Vision of Britain* to her. She loved to entertain and, while not as Bohemian as her wayward daughter Princess Margaret, would sprinkle people from the arts, such as Sir Roy Strong or Cecil Beaton, among the racing types and grandees she had to lunch.

Paul Goldberger, architecture critic of the *New York Times*, may not have been wide of the mark when he wrote:

> Charles's architectural education, one of his friends has remarked, consisted of 'looking out of the window of a Rolls-Royce listening to his mother and grandmother say, "Isn't all that ugly?"'

But then, except for the Rolls-Royce, that would have been true of many people. They did not like what they saw and were entitled to their view. Pursuing their uncomplaining round of opening public buildings and visiting places of work, the Royal Family saw more of Britain than any architect or journalist – and their range was not confined to the metropolis. They cannot have been blind to what had happened to the country's buildings since the Second World War.

Only the Queen's cousin the Duke of Gloucester has a training in architecture – but all the Royal Family read newspapers and magazines. Charles must have seen *Private Eye*, which was required reading for his generation at Cambridge and beyond; its humour was widely quoted at dinner parties and everyone in the swim knew the hilarious Dear Bill letters (purportedly written by Margaret Thatcher's husband, Denis). Since 1971 the magazine had been running a column called Nooks and Corners of the New Barbarism, founded by the poet John Betjeman and continued by his daughter Candida Lycett Green; the term New Barbarism was a dig at New Brutalism, the style of blocky, bunker-like buildings with walls of shuttered concrete displayed par excellence by the Hayward Gallery on London's South Bank. Lycett Green often took Charles, in a variety of hats and coats to provide a theatrical disguise, around the country, introducing him not only to the churches and gardens so beloved of her father but to creative friends, such as Isabel and Julian Bannerman, the gardeners who would create the stumpery at Highgrove.

In 1979, the astringent journalist and conservationist Gavin Stamp took over Lycett Green's column, now called just Nooks and Corners. Stamp was one of a small but vocal band informally known as the Young Fogeys, a group of cultural conservatives who dressed in corduroy trousers and the sort of Edwardian clothes that could then be bought in second-hand shops, and rode old-fashioned bikes with baskets on the front. All were architecturally aware, all conservationists, most belonged to amenity societies such as the Georgian Group, the Victorian Society and the Thirties Society, later renamed the Twentieth Century Society (founded in 1979). Many of the Young Fogeys wrote for the *Spectator*, *Country Life* and other publications, where Charles might have read them. He would also have known of 'The Destruction of the Country House' exhibition which opened at the Victoria and Albert Museum in 1974, documenting the hundreds of country houses that had been demolished over the previous century. If he went, it was incognito, but his mother was taken around by the director Sir Roy Strong, who remembers her as being 'a very sharp observer'.

The 'Destruction' exhibition led to the foundation of SAVE Britain's Heritage, a campaigning body whose prime mover was the indefatigable Marcus Binney, an architectural writer on *Country Life*. SAVE's gift for publicity gave conservation a high profile. In the same year, 1975, the late Colin Amery, who wrote a column on architecture for the *Financial Times*, and Dan Cruickshank, a journalist on the *Architectural Review*, published *The Rape of Britain*, drawing attention to the appalling levels of destruction that had been visited upon towns and cities since the 1950s. They were also prominent among the diehard conservationists of the Spitalfields Trust, founded to protect an area of beautiful Huguenot silk weavers' houses to the East of Liverpool Street station, then occupied by members of the Bangladeshi community. The distinguished architectural historian Mark Girouard was among a deputation to the offices of British Land who staged a sit-in to prevent the demolition of part of Elder Street in 1977. While few column inches were devoted to the critique of new architecture, newspapers found conservation to be a hot topic. This was illustrated when Trafalgar House smashed up the Art Deco façade of the Firestone Factory on the Great West Road in 1980, on the eve of its being listed: the outrage was universal. Campaigners were often journalists or had friends in the press. All the major newspapers had architectural correspondents to cover stories that were the stuff of dinner-party conversation.

In 1993, the Prince remembered 'the feeling of despair' he had suffered in the 1960s 'as I saw the remaining untouched wild places being progressively grubbed up and converted to agricultural production on an almost industrial basis'. One can imagine that the demolition of old buildings and their replacement by larger, unornamented structures built of industrially produced materials would have had a similar effect. This was happening everywhere in Britain, and nobody could have been more aware of it than Prince Charles, given his engagements around the country. Presumably he read the newspapers. Much as the Royal Family came to dislike the press, journalists were among the circle from whom the Prince sought advice, including Amery and Simon Jenkins. Both wrote drafts of speeches for Charles. Jenkins was eventually dropped when his work as a newspaper editor made him unavailable to the Prince – personal loyalty, if not patriotism itself, required court members to be permanently at the ready, whether or not they were paid (and many who gave expert advice on the Prince's enthusiasms weren't). Amery, however, succeeded in staying the course, being a consummate courtier – so consummate that sadly he left no record of his long involvement with the Prince and his charities at his death in 2018.

Although Prince Charles chose his advisors well, the ideas they helped him to articulate were not particularly original. That was the whole point. They were the sort of thing that people had been saying for years. What was novel was that they should have been uttered by the Prince of Wales. When they were, the architectural establishment, the government and sometimes even property developers – all of whom, it seemed, had been deaf to argument – had to open their ears.

The 'carbuncle affair', as Annan called it, revealed that Charles's words could influence events. In hunting terms, it was his first taste of blood. Where would hounds take him next?

TWO

PEOPLE

Community Architecture

'**A**SHORT MAN WITH NARROW-SET EYES AND A restless manner, in private Hackney's responses to challenging questions are delivered with self-sealing endings which announce that – to his mind – the last word has just been pronounced on the subject. He also tends to sweeten up a lull in the conversation by tossing in a reference to a Royal yacht or a Royal train.' That was how Rod Hackney struck the journalist and film director Peter Lennon, who wrote a profile of him in *The Listener* on December 4, 1986 under the headline 'GURU OF COMMUNITY ARCHITECTS'. Lennon does not seem to have warmed to 'a man of the kind of strutting confidence which eschews bashfulness'. Nevertheless the Prince of Wales took a shine to him. Having singled him out for praise in his Hampton Court speech, he made him his adviser on the problems of inner-city housing, recognising that poor housing was not only bad in itself but a factor in the alienation of the black and other ethnic communities, seen in Toxteth, Broadwater Farm and over 30 other riots that had taken place in 1981 and 1985. When, the day after the *Listener* profile appeared, Hackney defeated the

Aftermath of the 1985 riots on the Broadwater Farm estate in Tottenham, North London. Rioting symbolised the disintegration of Britain's inner cities, which Prince Charles sought to counter.

establishment candidate to become President of the RIBA, it seemed that an alternative force in architecture was on the verge of a breakthrough.

Hackney was not an obvious candidate to join the royal circle. Born in Liverpool during the Blitz, he was the son of a dancer and a hotel chef. When he was five, the family settled in North Wales where his father had work. At school, lessons were given in Welsh, a language the young Rod could not speak. He took refuge in art, a subject in which he could shine. In due course, art would lead him to study architecture, there being no requirement to have a maths A-level in those days (Hackney did not even have an O-level in maths). Entering Manchester University in 1961, Hackney was, he remembers, 'among the first students to receive a training devoted entirely to Modernism'. Nearly 30 years later he published a perceptive critique of Modernism in his book *The Good, the Bad and the Ugly: Cities in Crisis.*

> Modernism has failed in its primary aim to improve the lives of ordinary people. It attempted to achieve too much too quickly. Mass-scale planning did away with traditional urban lifestyles and street patterns. Mass production and standardization produced bland, often poorly constructed buildings. Technology was pushed beyond its limits, which led to major structural weaknesses. The new materials laid Modernism open to abuse by get-rich-quick developers and people's needs were left behind in the rush. At its best Modernism has worked spectacularly well – when small-scale and well built – but it simply does not work in any context in the hands of second-raters. While the man and woman in the street have long been questioning the merits of the new-style architecture, the design profession only really began to smart when Prince Charles launched his attack on contemporary building.

These ideas began to germinate, Hackney remembers, during his years at Manchester. While other students chose the gods of the Modernist pantheon as their heroes, Hackney preferred the Victorian engineer Thomas Telford, remarkable for the London-to-Holyhead road and numerous bridges, but unsexy. Le Corbusier's chapel at Ronchamp in Eastern France seemed an exciting piece of architecture, but his proposals for mass housing disastrous.

Hackney's first jobs were abroad; he worked in Canada, Libya and, for two years, for Arne Jacobsen, whose Kuwait Central Bank was capable of withstanding nuclear attack. With a dome covered in gold leaf, it was reputed to be the world's costliest building. His return to Manchester in 1971, to write a PhD on Jacobsen, was a contrast. He became absorbed in the battles of local residents' groups wanting to keep their supposedly insanitary terraced homes in the face of slum clearance. Almost 90,000 homes in the city had already been bulldozed. Some might have suffered bomb damage but, as Hackney wrote later,

> Hitler hadn't caused a fraction of the destruction which followed in his wake under the guidance of Alf Young – Manchester City Council's energetic chief public health officer ... anything built before 1919 was by definition a slum and had to go.

Alas, the urban renewal projects which replaced the terraces were not only soulless but afflicted with a myriad of problems, such as – to name only one – infestation by pests. Rats gnawed the plastic pipe insulation, cockroaches thrived in the ventilation system and fleas multiplied behind wallpaper and timber skirting. 'Fumigation was easy in a Victorian house. But with large blocks all the flats linked together in one area had to be evacuated before any treatment could be considered.'

Hackney acquired a personal stake in the fight against redevelopment when, to save money that he would otherwise have spent on rent, he bought a two-up two-down house in Black Road, Macclesfield, built for workers in the nearby brick factory in 1815. Facilities in the street were basic. Hackney's house was unusual in having an indoor lavatory, but he had to wash outside. It was an attempt to secure a £20 grant towards the cost of installing a washbasin in 1972 that led to his first great contest with officialdom, on behalf of an established community of residents who did not want decisions about their cherished homes to be handed down from above. Initially, Hackney's grant application was refused, on the grounds that the street would be demolished in five or ten years' time. As Hackney remembers,

'The corporation was proud of its modern approach.' It had recently completed a number of big block schemes, including an immense development called Victoria Park behind the four-storey, glass and cast-iron warehouse by Macclesfield's railway station, built by Arigi Bianchi and Company in 1892; Harold Wilson's housing minister, Anthony Greenwood, called it 'the finest housing development in the country'. (Arigi Bianchi still stands after 130 years, Victoria Park was demolished in 2000–02 after little more than 30 years.) However, Hackney's architectural training enabled him to argue that the terraces on Black Road were basically sound, just poorly maintained and unmodernised. The local MP, who was more familiar with the provisions of the 1969 Housing Act than the council, was recruited to the cause. He helped to get the street redesignated as a General Improvement Area. It turned out that the lady who owned five of the Black Road properties lived in North Wales off the meagre rents from her houses but was too poor to maintain them. Preferring a lump sum to the dribble of rental income, she was persuaded to sell up; a means was found by which the tenants could buy their homes; and the pattern was repeated elsewhere along the street.

Hackney's handiwork turned his own property into a show home, to demonstrate to the authorities what could be done. Hackney was appointed architect to Black Road's attempt to improve itself. Most of the work was done by the residents. In May 1974, *Building Design* reported progress:

> Self-help improvement under GIA is cheaper, more effective and environmentally less polluting than the simplistic expensive local authority clearance renewal programmes … In Black Road the motto is small is beautiful. Participants, from pensioners to unmarried mothers, are happy. The contractors are happy. Rod Hackney is happy and Macclesfield is happy.

Dr Rod Hackney, champion of Community Architecture, at Macclesfield, in Cheshire. Behind him to the left is the old Hovis Mill, converted to apartments in the 1990s; to the right is part of Black Road, whose self-help revival in the face of council attempts to demolish it established his reputation.

Community Architecture had triumphed.

Prince Charles had visited Black Road in February 1984, shortly before giving the Hampton Court speech. Hackney's approach struck a chord with him. Perhaps the self-help element evoked memories of his mother's practical, make-do-and-mend attitude to her domestic surroundings, celebrated in Mary Killen's 2020 book *What Would HM the Queen Do?*, and the Queen Mother's affection for homespun pleasures, which would be such a feature of the 100th birthday pageant held in her honour in 2000: 'like a village fete on a larger scale,' as William Rees-Mogg described it in *The Times*. More importantly, it offered hope of ameliorating the urgent social issues with which the Prince was now engaged. 'It goes back years,' said Harold Haywood, director of the Royal

Jubilee and Prince's Trusts, speaking of the Prince's concern for the youth in inner cities, after a midnight visit Prince Charles had made to dossers 'in urine-soaked blankets' on London's South Bank in 1985.

> From when we had the first disturbances in his wedding year, 1981, His Royal Highness has been very concerned to ask what we could do in cooperation with others to alleviate stress and help the young.

Inner-city regeneration was a theme of both trusts. Travelling the country on his royal duties, the Prince could see at first hand the misery caused by bad housing schemes and devastated city centres; his intuition that these rips in the social fabric, expressed in the abject failure of so many architectural projects since the Second World War, were contributary causes of the rioting of the early 1980s was being confirmed by government studies. 'A number of researchers, including those in a team working for the Home Office, are already convinced of the link between housing estate design and disorder, vandalism and crime,' wrote *The Sunday Times*'s Week in Focus team. In 1985 the idea was given academic credibility by Alice Coleman, then a lecturer in the geography department of King's College, London and soon to be a professor, in her book *Utopia on Trial*. British planning was 'born with a mission to clear slums and create a modern urban fabric to engender stable, contented and crime-free communities. Unfortunately,' she wrote in the journal of the Town and Country Planning Association, May 1986,

> this has rarely been achieved ... [Instead,] the crime rate has risen inexorably, vandalism has become rife, and many kinds of social breakdown, from divorce to drugtaking, have

multiplied. Furthermore, there is growing evidence that all these problems are most concentrated in the planned town-scape that differs most dramatically from the unplanned traditional streetscape of the past.

It is in areas of extensive redevelopment and unfortunate neighbouring areas of crime overspill that insurance companies have imposed a massive increase in premiums, with the result that householders not only have to suffer the social injury of misconceived planning – they have to pay extra for it as well.

As president of the Prince's Foundation for the Built Environment, Prince Charles visits an old maltings in Mistley, Essex, in 2004, to show his support for the restoration.

When overhead walkways were removed from Westminster City Council's Lisson Green Estate, the crime rate was halved. The division of estates into separate sections, each with only one entrance so that strangers could not wander through, could have dramatic consequences: two ground-floor families on an estate in Southwark 'who had boarded up their windows and lived in artificial light for years, quickly felt sufficiently secure and relaxed to take down the boarding'. Fear of crime could be almost as damaging as crime itself.

Part of the problem could have been that tenants of large-scale council projects felt they had lost control of their surroundings. Decisions that affected their everyday existence might be taken by remote and inefficient property managers, who could all too easily give the impression that they did not care. Hence the Prince's desire, expressed in 1987, to 'jump feet first into the kind of spaghetti Bolognese of red tape which clogs this country from one end to the other'. On the face of it, the Prince had picked an unlikely, if fashionable, target: bureaucracy was a bête noire of Thatcherite free marketeers who saw it as a choke on economic growth; it was a curse of the European Community. Business, however, was not what the Prince had in mind – some would have said it rarely was; nor Brussels. His target was the bureaucratic small-mindedness that bred in council offices, where box-ticking officials could make the life of council tenants hell. Advised by Hackney, the Prince toured as much Community Architecture as he could. The itinerary included Utopia Village off Regent's Park, in London – an unexpected destination since its architect was Richard Burton, one of the partners in ABK, architects of the carbuncle scheme at the National Gallery. The Prince was trying to make up.

Hackney, who may be said to have benefitted from ABK's discomfiture, did not himself last long near the sun. Although he

This photograph of 1992 shows Prince Charles having tea with tenants of a Battersea development. The Community Architecture that he supported depended on patient architects investigating the needs of tenants, often over interminable cups of tea.

remained President of the RIBA until 1989, the truth was that he had fallen from grace before his term had even started. It was both a strength and a weakness of a royal dilettante such as Charles that he could take people up when they interested him, and drop them without ceremony when another candidate for his attention came along, or when a favourite transgressed against one of the many unspoken codes. For the naïve, who thought they had found a friend for life, this could be hurtful. On the other hand, anyone should have known that while the Prince met more people in a year than anyone in the country, very few of them entered the inner circle of friendship, most of whose members – generally Etonians, likely to own a country estate – he had known a long time. They were tried, trusted and (an essential qualification) discreet. Hackney's downfall came as a direct result of his love of name-dropping remarks about the Royal yacht and Royal train. Interviewed by the *Manchester Evening News*, he shared views expressed by the Prince during a private dinner on the train after the Handsworth riots, during which four people died:

> He is very worried that when he becomes king there will be 'no go' areas in the inner cities and that the minorities will be alienated from the rest of the country.

The Prince, then on a tour of Australia and the United States with Princess Diana, was said, by other newspapers, 'to feel betrayed'. Hackney was sent a letter of rebuke. Rightly, the Prince feared that the indiscretion would compromise the Royal Family's carefully nurtured position above politics; indeed the Shadow Home Secretary Gerald Kaufman, a Manchester MP, lost no time in quoting Hackney's words in Parliament. The Prince was also said to find the words put into his mouth, 'when I become king', pompous and distasteful. There was no way back from a gaffe of this magnitude. Hackney was metaphorically ejected from the train.[1]

Perhaps Hackney's days were already numbered. The Prince did not lessen his belief in public consultation – it matured into method known as Enquiry-by-Design, a series of intense workshops that would be held by the architects of the Prince of Wales's Institute of Architecture, later the Prince's Foundation (and now the King's Foundation) as part of the design process. But he may already have seen its limitations as a route to producing the best architecture. Gavin Stamp lambasted its inadequacy in typically scathing terms:

> Dr Hackney's twee little brick houses in Macclesfield look very different from the extraordinary Byker Wall in Newcastle,

a housing complex looking like a Tibetan Monastery which was designed by Ralph Erskine in 1972 after consultation with displaced local residents … Unfortunately, [Hackney's] restored terraces merely look as if they had been done over by enthusiastic DIY owners in the spirit of Barry Bucknell [presenter of the BBC TV series *Barry Bucknell's Do It Yourself*]. The architectural character of the houses has been spoiled, but Hackney says that does not matter: what matters is that tenants or owners should have done what they want.

This may have been intellectually arrogant of Dr Stamp, a Cambridge PhD, but he had identified the aesthetic weakness of Community Architecture.

By 1988, even Hackney was happy to admit that 'it had lost its radical edge'. But the movement, bolstered by the Prince, had forced architects to put their egos aside and look more intently at the needs of the people who would inhabit their buildings. The social housing that is now being designed by Peter Barber and Mikhail Riches is infinitely better than the generality of that produced during the post-Second World War decades; it is impossible to quantify how much the Prince's involvement may have contributed to this improvement but his intervention undoubtedly helped the process along. And Black Road, Macclesfield may have another lesson to teach. Built during the Regency, its unpretentious houses were inherently pleasant and dignified. No architect had been near them at the time they were designed. But their proportions conformed to a tradition that stretched back more than 2,000 years, transmitting the wisdom and experience of generations, from the Ancient World into our own. This was Classicism. It would be the Prince's next big thing.

THREE

CLASSICISM

Paternoster Square and The Mansion House Speech

I N 1980, THE DUCHY OF CORNWALL BOUGHT CHARLES a country house in the expectation that he would soon fulfil the nation's hopes and get married, which he did the next year. This was Highgrove House outside Tetbury, probably built by the Gloucestershire architect Anthony Keck in the 1790s. Originally, Highgrove had been an elegant if austere Neo-Classical box, but a fire had ripped through it in 1893 and the restoration had been in a heavier style. A wing added at that time had been reduced in the 1960s. Charles's immediate concern was the garden. It took him longer to address the architecture. Although some critics, if they knew of the house, admired Keck's restraint, the effect was insufficiently princely for a man who had grown up in palaces. For advice, he did not turn to an architect but to Felix Kelly, a New Zealander who had served in the RAF before becoming, with little artistic training, 'one of the most gifted, knowledgeable and prolific recorders of English and North American country houses' of the 20th century. Born in 1914, Kelly had a dreamily nostalgic style, perfectly suited to the romanticism of the early years of Elizabeth II's reign, when Norman

Hartnell made the Queen's dresses in the New Look; it had not changed. He painted a major scheme of murals at Castle Howard, newly rebuilt after a fire; but more relevant to Highgrove was a painting he made for the industrialist Sebastian de Ferranti, showing a version of Palladio's Villa Rotonda – this was the inspiration for Henbury Hall in Cheshire, to be executed, with refinements, by the Classical architect Julian Bicknell. At Highgrove, he proposed adding a pediment, replacing the heavy parapet with a balustrade, and rebuilding the wing; all this would be detailed, on the builders' recommendation, by Peter Falconer, an industrial architect. Although Falconer had no great interest in Classical architecture, he was able to provide an engineering solution to the problem of the balustrade, which would have revealed an ugly stepped gutter if action had not been taken. As his *Times* obituary records,

> Falconer's master stroke was to find a firm in Dursley that was able to fashion a new gutter consisting of shallow glass-fibre trays, still stepping down to the corners but invisible behind the new balustrade. Following Kelly's suggestion, Falconer also added the pilasters to the front. These he detailed with scholarly care and precision.

The work took place in 1987.

Inside the rooms had been decorated at the time of the Prince's marriage by Dudley Poplak, a suggestion of Princess Diana's mother, Frances Shand Kydd, in what he called 'a youthful variant of the chintzy country-house look that was seen everywhere that year'; as his *Times* obituary noted on March 29, 2005, the Princess was 'possibly his only client who was still a teenager at the time of his commission'. Poplak became a trusted friend who would exchange letters with both the Prince and the Princess as their marriage failed, loading the latter with philosophical books that might help her through the ordeal. 'You are marvellous, Dudley, the way you've kindly sent me all these things to read – they do interest me enormously,' she wrote from Kensington Palace on February 1, 1992. Later Poplak's clean, fresh lime green and aquamarine would be replaced by Robert Kime in a masculine, broadly Regency style that combined beautiful objects from the Royal Collection with rich fabrics and comfort.

It was not much noticed at the time, but the Prince's work on his house showed a change of direction. Community Architecture had convinced him of the importance of consulting the different parties who would be affected by an architectural project before it began. In the case of public housing, this was only considerate and humane; but the principle applied to commercial projects of all kinds, too. The Prince, like others in his family, was keen on consensus and had used his position to bring apparently irreconcilable factions together to promote social harmony, an early example being a meeting between disaffected young black people in South London and the police in 1977, which he personally chaired at Buckingham Palace.[1] Clearly it was better that an architectural development should benefit as many parties as possible – and besides, there was the planning system to propitiate: vociferous objections could delay if not scupper a scheme, however well-intentioned. But Community Architecture had run its course for the Prince. Done properly, it took up an impractical amount of the architect's time; this made it uneconomic. Few architects make large fortunes, but even fewer are saintly enough to spend their lives in endless discussion with residents' associations, revising their plans over cups of tea. They want to design; that is why they go into the profession. Besides, the Prince could see the truth of Gavin Stamp's criticism quoted earlier: the results were visually uninspiring. By contrast, the terraces of Georgian London had been rolled out quickly, one after another, on a speculative basis; and they were now a joy to live in and stroll through. Edinburgh New Town was full of monuments that formed a splendid background to daily life. What was it that united these and other places to which the Prince intuitively responded, designed by architects who were not of the first rank – sometimes not architects at all but mere builders – but nevertheless designed well? They were in the Classical tradition, that broad river that had been flowing from the wellsprings of the Ancient World since the 5th century BC. Classicism is dead, said the Modernists. That was not quite true, but it was certainly on its last legs. Could it yet be revived?

Here was a radical idea. To achieve his hope, the Prince would have to find some young architects mad enough to devote their lives to a movement which offered little prospect of getting work. The link with the last generation of architects who designed in the Classical style had been all but broken. In the 1950s, Vincent Harris, McMorran & Whitby and John Brandon-Jones had all built civic buildings in a manner loosely derived, via the Arts and Crafts Movement, from Wren. Budgets were tight, building materials inferior, detail thin, but Brandon-Jones had succeeded in erecting his Staines Council Offices in Surrey – brick with a tower and hipped, clay-tiled roofs and an arcaded loggia on the ground floor – as late as 1972. Now Brandon-Jones was in his late-80s; Vincent Harris, Donald McMorran and George Whitby were all dead.

Before the Second World War, Modernism had been a cult, foreign in origin and patronised by intellectuals. After the War, it swept the board. Proponents could argue that not only was it more rational – cheaper – to build in mass-produced materials but it better suited the priorities of the age. It was the outward symbol of a more egalitarian society, whose needs would be met by the caring hands of the State. Culturally, the axis had shifted.

No longer did Britain look to Continental Europe for inspiration, but to the United States, the land of opportunity which had come out of the War so much richer than anyone else. In fact, architecture in America was not as ideologically dogmatic as it became in the UK, and Classicism was never entirely dislodged from the public mind as the appropriate style for public buildings; the tribal memory of New England churches, the Greek Revival of the Federal period and the Beaux-Arts swank of the Gilded Age was too strong. But British architects and planners were blind to the pluralism of the US; to them and others, America was a symbol of exuberant modernity. Plate glass and reinforced concrete typified everything that was go-ahead, everything that was functional and well-heated in the land where ordinary people (at a time of food rationing in Britain) could eat steak.

The best of the Classicists was Raymond Erith, who retreated from London on grounds of taste and cost to Dedham, in the Constable country of North Essex; like Francis Johnson, his Yorkshire counterpart, he would not have been able to survive on the income derived from the modest commissions that came his way, had it not been for a private income. He died in 1973, when the economic and political outlook for Britain was at its bleakest following the Oil Crisis.

Unusually discriminating and inventive, Erith had been, in one way, typical of his time: he accepted the rationale for Modernism and dreamt that an accommodation might be found between its structural principles and his own Classicism. This was not the view of the man who took over the practice, Quinlan Terry. Terry had no truck with compromise. To him, Classical architecture did not just mean a system of proportion or a repertoire of ornament but a way of building. Walls should be of load-bearing masonry, urns carved of stone. There was so little work to be had during his first years in practice that he could spend them decorating his

This perspective by Carl Laubin shows the first John Simpson scheme for Paternoster Square, which was exhibited in the crypt of St Paul's Cathedral. An accompanying poster succinctly expressed the Prince's philosophy: 'Make Street and Squares that Everyone can Enjoy.' The scheme proved popular with the public who visited.

Suffolk home with *trompe l'oeil* murals and making linocuts. But his fortunes changed during the Thatcher decade, when clients included the Environment Secretary Michael Heseltine and the Conservative Party Treasurer Alistair McAlpine; they were standard bearers for the revival not just of Britain's economy but a way of life that put the fruits of capitalism on show. Rich, private clients – but Terry reached beyond them, taking the fight to Modernism on its own turf, by designing a large office development at Richmond Riverside on the Thames, opened by HM The Queen in 1988. A monolithic Modernist scheme had previously been rejected for this sensitive site. Terry replaced it with a row of different offices each expressed in a different Classical idiom, in the manner of an architectural caprice. The Prince would meet, admire and sometimes correspond with Terry, who was the most prominent of the few Classical architects in the country. But it would not be Terry who led the charge at Charles's next public intervention: Paternoster Square.

For there also existed a tiny cell of young architectural refuse-niks who, to the puzzlement of their tutors at architectural school, would not toe the Modernist line. They were as yet unknown to the wider public and had built little. Work for all architects was scarce during the recession of the early 1980s. But this provided them with an opportunity; with nothing else on their hands, they decided to publicise their ideas. Robert Adam turned to journalism, while John Simpson organised an exhibition called *Classical Survival, Classical Revival*, showing the work of 20 mostly Classical architects ('mostly' because to get to that number it was necessary to include some who were traditionalists or even Gothic Revivalists). Simpson had originally thought the show might consist simply of drawings displayed on the staircase of his 18th-century office in Great James Street, Bloomsbury. Encouraged to apply for a grant from, improbably, the Greater London

Council – then, under Ken Livingstone, a bastion of socialist ideology, which would not have been expected to favour a style generally associated with elite country houses – he obtained £500. It was enough for him to transfer the exhibition to the Building Centre on Store Street. This was followed by another exhibition on the same theme, more generously mounted: provocatively named *Real Architecture*, it opened in March 1987.

The organisers, who had been doing it for their own amusement as much as anything, were surprised by the extent of publicity that the exhibitions achieved. They took place in a now forgotten age when all the major newspapers regarded the architectural debate as an important subject to cover. It was regularly featured in *The Times*, *Daily Telegraph*, *Guardian* and *Financial Times* as well as the Sunday papers and *Country Life*. The reception given to the New Classicism, as it became known, was mixed – critics close to the architectural profession hated it, those who wrote for the public at large were often enthusiastic. Charles Knevitt of *The Times*, not known as a traditionalist (although it is claimed that he coined the term Community Architecture), gave the exhibition an unexpectedly rave review:

> The return of classicism may be seen as an inevitable conse-
> quence of the public's rejection of much of what has been
> built in post-war Britain: the unacceptable face of architecture
> represented by the municipal macho and commercial materi-
> alism which has torn the soul out of many of our towns and
> cities and made them a wasteland.
>
> In the 50 years since the Modern Movement in architecture
> arrived on our shores through the influence of architectural
> refugees from Europe, the profession has failed to formulate
> a new language that is acceptable to the public.

Lessons about proportion, scale, texture, ornament and colour, and the use of materials which mature with age and require the minimum of maintenance, were forgotten or abandoned in the quest for innovation.

Only now are we once more designing buildings which respect their context as well as the spirit of the age.

Word had already reached the Prince of Wales: he opened the show.

1987 would be a big year. During it, the Prince was approached by Lady Wynne-Jones, the large, unstoppable widow of a Labour peer and chairwoman of the London Society, who had once threatened to champion one of her causes by imitating Lady Godiva's naked ride (the Palace had attempted to stop her linking the Prince's name with her activities, to no avail). A self-confessed 'volcano' of opposition to tall buildings, she was concerned by a plan to replace Paternoster Square next to St Paul's Cathedral. Paternoster – the Latin for 'Our Father', the first words of the Lord's Prayer – is an ancient name: in Pepys's day, Paternoster Row was the place to find booksellers and printers, who had been plying their trade near the cathedral since the 16th century because of the demand for religious books. But the area was largely burnt out during the Blitz by incendiary bombs aimed at St Paul's – in the effort to protect it, on Churchill's personal orders, all the available fire engines had their hoses trained on its walls, to the sacrifice of lesser streets. Still, the nearby buildings had only been burnt, not destroyed: the shells survived and it would have been possible to rebuild some of them. But the decision was taken to make a clean sweep. The medieval street plan, which had survived Wren's attempts to reform it after the Great Fire of London, was cleared away, along with the remains of the architecture. To the north of the cathedral, a large triangular site was replaced by Sir William (later Baron) Holford with a layout that might have been made on a piece of graph paper – all straight lines and right angles. This was Paternoster Square.

Born in South Africa, Holford had come to England in 1925. Having studied under the Beaux-Arts Classicist Professor Charles Reilly at Liverpool, he went to Rome for three years – but by now he had discovered Le Corbusier. During the Second World War, he was made principal adviser to the new Ministry of Town and Country Planning; after that he became one of the two

After the Second World War, the planner Lord Holford obliterated the medieval street plan around St Paul's, as well as the shells of the Victorian buildings that had been gutted during the Blitz, replacing it with a raised piazza surrounded by shoebox-like buildings. Finished in the late 1960s, the inflexible scheme had to be replaced within 20 years.

planning consultants to the City of London, which had been devastated by bombing. Planners were in demand in the post-war years as Britain repaired war damage and attempted to provide better housing amid road systems suitable for the motor car. His St Paul's scheme deliberately avoided any reference to the character of the old townscape, which had developed incrementally over centuries – 'no harmony of scale, character, or placing, just a total contrast'.

Sweeping away the medieval street pattern, Paternoster Square was not a conventional square but a raised piazza where pedestrians could access four high-rise office blocks from walkways, leaving the ground level to traffic. Strangely, for all that Modernism deplored architectural dishonesty, the material that these buildings displayed to the world was not concrete, but a fine and expensive imitation of it made from Portland stone. Fresh from the quarry, this new stone was gleaming white, whereas the walls of the cathedral were black from centuries of smoke from coal fires – though in the mid 1960s the cathedral was cleaned.

Rising to a maximum of 16 storeys, the towers provided less office space than the Victorian buildings of four or five storeys which had preceded them. In that sense it was idealistic. After the War, Britain was desperate for renewal, the City wanted to get back to work quickly, and some people actively hated the Victorian past whose built legacy of crockets and spires seemed as outdated as the hansom cab. These factors help explain why the City authorities allowed Paternoster Square to be built. But it was never loved. 'The quality of Holford's planning round the cathedral was let down by impoverished commercial architecture,' observes Mervyn Miller in Holford's entry in the *Oxford Dictionary of National Biography*. 'Its mediocre, windswept squares never gained public acclaim.'

Begun in 1961, Paternoster Square was not finished until 1967.

'New Ball Game'. Louis Hellman's cartoon from the *Architects' Journal*, June 1988, shows Arup, about to be awarded the prize of Paternoster Square, being told that they have been thwarted. Prince Charles wants his own player (John Simpson, shown left) to play under new rules, with himself as umpire.

A mere 20 years later, Holford's vision of what the future would be had been overtaken by events: low-ceilinged offices on the shallow floor plate that had been standard before the advent of air conditioning became unlettable after Big Bang, when businesses wanted trading floors with computer cabling hidden below. One of the disadvantages of the Modernist steel frame is that the buildings that it supports are inflexible and cannot easily be changed to meet different needs. So the Mountleigh Group, which had acquired most of the site, deemed that it had to come down. It organised a limited competition between eight Modernist firms, including Richard Rogers, to find a replacement. Rogers did not win on this occasion; the laurels went instead to Arup Associates.

Needing to maximise the lettable space, their scheme was out of scale. It was also lacklustre. Lady Wynne-Jones deplored it and said so to the Prince at a Palace soirée.

As Jonathan Dimbleby has described, the Prince swung into action. In Britain you do not have to own a parcel of land to apply for planning permission on it; anyone can do that. John Simpson was prevailed upon to see if he would produce an alternative scheme to Arup's. This was an extraordinarily bold proposition. Simpson was then in his late-20s; his oeuvre did not extend very far beyond a villa in Sussex, ingenious, heavily influenced by his hero Soane but not large, for his parents. Here he was being asked to plan and design one of the most important urban sites in the country. Admittedly there was no immediate prospect of its being built, nor even money to meet the office costs. Initially Simpson demurred – not from lack of confidence but because the project would have been too much for his fledgling practice to bear. But Mira Bar-Hillel, the *Evening Standard*'s architecture critic, took it to her editor, John Leese, to see if the *Standard* would underwrite the campaign. Leese said that it would, and Simpson hurried into action. He not only designed a new square in the centre of which would be a market building, akin to the one at Covent Garden, providing access to a lower level of shops leading to the entrance to St Paul's Underground station, but looked at the entire setting of the cathedral, much of which was due to be rebuilt in coming years. Rather than concentrating the office space in a small number of towers, Simpson distributed it among a larger number of Victorian-scale buildings, with cornices and classical ornament, made from the traditional materials of stone, brick, slate, tile and copper. Visits to Highgrove and St James's Palace kept the Prince abreast of progress.

In 1984, the Prince's opinions about Modernism were largely his own, and intuitive. By the summer of 1987, his Deputy Private

Secretary Humphrey Mews had realised he would need expert advice if he was to continue to remain engaged with the theme. Around the time of the Hampton Court speech, the Prince had met Jules Lubbock, an art historian from that hotbed of radicalism, the University of Essex, housed since its opening in 1964 in just the sort of buildings that the Prince detested. (The architect explained his aesthetic by saying: 'The English love making things shaggy and softening everything up. We decided to do something fierce to let them work within.' After Christmas 1962 he presented the Vice-Chancellor, Albert Sloman, with a model made from his son's Lego set.) Except for its architecture, the campus was Lubbock's natural habitat. Not only was he 'the archetypal scruffy young academic' but the architecture critic of the leftist *New Statesman* – hardly the sort of person you would have expected the Prince to take to his bosom. But they 'seemed to hit it off,' according to an insider, and Lubbock became the Prince's sounding board for the rest of the 1980s. 'The destruction of the once-magnificent London skyline, centering on the dome of St Paul's,' reads one of Lubbock's *New Statesman* columns in June 1987,

> was a grotesque accident; one which resulted from bad planning legislation as surely as traffic accidents result from bad roads.

At the time it seemed like an eccentric one-man campaign, but it chimed with the Prince.

It was to Lubbock that Mews turned when he wanted to create an Architectural Advisory Group after the Prince's office was flooded with requests for support following the 'carbuncle' speech. At that time, the gang consisted initially of Candida Lycett Green, Christopher Martin, who would later make the

Prince's television documentary *A Vision of Britain*, and the sculptor, editor and renegade Modernist-turned-Classicist Theo Crosby. (Rather grandly the journalist Christopher Booker declined to join.) The original core would be joined on an ad hoc basis by the planning lawyer Jeremy Sullivan QC, the antiques dealer and man of taste Christopher Gibbs, the mysticist and sacred geometer Keith Critchlow, and Colin Amery. A younger figure was Giles Worsley, architectural editor of *Country Life*, who would go on to edit the Prince's ill-fated venture into magazine journalism, *Perspectives*. The group's initially part-time secretary was Brian Hanson who would be a linchpin of the Prince's architectural operations for a decade. On a warm September afternoon, it met at Highgrove. The Prince had flown down from Balmoral to join them. Rod Hackney arrived by helicopter. Others who joined the party were said to be Léon Krier, the Luxembourgish theorist and masterplanner, and Jeremy Benson, the chairman of the Georgian Group. Crosby said his main recollection was less of the conversation than of the sound of helicopters and lawnmowers.

By December 1 Simpson's proposal was ready and waiting, and the Prince of Wales could deliver a carefully crafted speech at the Mansion House. Addressing the assembled dignitaries of the City of London, including Stuart Lipton, the lead developer at Paternoster Square, the Prince quickly cut to the chase. 'Countless people are appalled by what has happened to their capital city, but feel totally powerless to do anything about it.' Nowhere was worse than the area around St Paul's Cathedral. In the space of a mere 15 years after the end of the War:

> the planners, architects and developers of the City wrecked the London skyline and desecrated the dome of St Paul's ... And at street level, just look at Paternoster Square! Did

modern planners and architects in London ever use their eyes? Those planners swept away the lanes and alleys, hidden-away squares and courtyards which in most other European countries would have been lovingly rebuilt after the War.

In Continental Europe many countries had taken great care to rebuild the damaged fabric of their cities, so that it reflected, if it did not replace, what had been lost. Not in London. 'Here, even the street where Shakespeare and Milton brought their manuscripts, the legendary Paternoster Row, "The Row", the very heart of publishing since Elizabethan times, was turned into a concrete service road leading to an underground car park!' From this he moved to another brickbat that soon became lodged in public consciousness.

You have, ladies and gentlemen, to give this much to the Luftwaffe: when it knocked down our buildings, it didn't replace them with anything more offensive than rubble. We did that. Clausewitz called war the continuation of diplomacy by other means. Around St Paul's, planning turned out to be the continuation of war by other means.

Fortunately, changing needs for commercial space had given the City another chance, with the imminent demolition of Holford's scheme. He urged that this 'heaven-sent opportunity to build a model of real quality, of excellence, next to so great a building, in the heart of our capital city' should not be lost.

The speech was even more full of content than his previous one. This is the more remarkable given what we now know of the private turmoil of his marriage. Clearly the Prince had found the time to think carefully about what he wanted to say, and how to say it best. Most of his message related to Paternoster Square. He made no bones about the dreariness of the competition. When invited by Lipton to comment on the seven finalists, he found that they had been confronted by a strictly commercial brief, whose prime aim was to maximise the amount of office space that could be delivered within the planning constraints.

> Surely here, if anywhere, was the time and place to sacrifice some profit, if need be, for generosity of vision, for elegance, for dignity; for buildings which would raise our spirits and our faith in commercial enterprise and prove that capitalism can have a human face, instead of that of a robot or word processor.

Generally, it was only the developer of a scheme who took the initiative, commissioning designs of which the public was in ignorance until they were submitted for planning approval. Should they be refused after all the hoops had been jumped through, up to a public inquiry, the developer would be free to make another submission. Knowing that a people's scheme for Paternoster Square was already in the wings, he called for an exhibition where the public could have their say: 'Is it right that the people, their elected representatives, the Secretary of State himself, can take no initiative of their own? Is it sensible that they can only react to developers' proposals?' Since the competition entries had merely been the architects' first thoughts, he called for an exhibition, which might include the designs of Wren, Hawksmoor and Lutyens as well as the present plans. 'But please, let it not be based on "overriding commercial considerations" – at least not in this part of the city.'

What was his own vision for the area?

> It should be a beautiful area on a human scale, built at ground level, not on top of a car park square, with small shops and

businesses at ground level ... I would like to see the mediaeval street plan of pre-war Paternoster reconstructed, not out of mere nostalgia, but to give meaning to surviving fragments like Amen Court and the Chapter House, now left like dispossessed refugees in an arid desert of God-forsaken buildings. I would like to see a roofscape that gives the impression that St Paul's is floating above it like a great ship on the sea. I would also like to see the kinds of materials Wren might have used – soft red brick and stone dressings, perhaps, and the ornament and detail of classical architecture, but on a scale humble enough not to compete with the monumentality of St Paul's.

I would like to see architects working with artists and craftsmen, showing that pleasure and delight are indeed returning to architecture after their long exile.

That is precisely what he had already seen in the Simpson scheme. He could see no reason

why wealth should not finance beauty that is in harmony with tradition, today as in the past. People too easily forget that the London of Wren's time was the greatest trading empire the world has ever seen. Yet it was of such a splendour that the vista Canaletto painted surpassed ancient Rome and even rivalled that of his own native city of Venice, itself a centre of world trade, and one which knew so well how the fruits of commerce should be celebrated in the arts and architecture.

Immediately after the speech, Simpson made his design public. Lipton gave the Prince the exhibition he had called for; it would take place in a crowded space – given that all the entries would be shown – in the crypt of St Paul's. To the original seven designs were added the Simpson scheme, to test public reaction. This played to Simpson's strengths. He was a natural polemicist. He also understood how to convince the public with beautiful images that looked like real buildings. So as well as two large paintings by the perspectivist Carl Laubin, he had commissioned an elegant model of his design in the context of St Paul's. Here were buildings that the public could immediately see and relate to, standing clearly in the Classical tradition that had been dominant in City architecture from the age of Wren until the last phase of Lutyens's Midland Bank head office on Poultry (now The Ned) was opened in 1939. Arup's model, by contrast, looked weird. The only building on their scale model was St Paul's, represented by the dome supported, to quote Richard Littlejohn in the *Evening Standard*,

> on some transparent plastic stilts. The surrounding area on the board is as barren as the Sahara, except for a few coloured lines and arrows. (The man who makes the papier maché must have been on a day off.) A few lumps of foam hang confusingly on the walls.

Simpson still has the books that he cleverly provided for the public to leave comments in. 'A tragic misguided travesty!' fumed an Honorary Fellow of the RIBA. 'We want/need a City suitable for the 3rd Millennium.' But for every rant of that kind there are many more votes of praise. 'I work here!' exclaimed one admirer. To another,

> The Simpson scheme is the only one I could bear to contemplate … Hopefully, hopefully a miracle will happen & it will be built!

With the wind already in its sails, the Simpson scheme was given further momentum by another exhibition. This was held at the Victoria and Albert Museum, an altogether different space from the crypt of St Paul's, and complemented the Prince's television programme, *A Vision of Britain*; it opened on September 7, 1989. In the centre of the show, pride of place was given to another Simpson model. This was an advance on the teaser exhibited at St Paul's, since it illustrated a fully worked-up scheme that could be submitted to the City of London for planning approval. Rather than looking at the context of St Paul's in the round, it focused on Paternoster Square itself. The previous model had imagined that the lines of the medieval precinct could be reinstated. By contrast, this one accepted the footprint of the Holford's development – too difficult to change because of ownership considerations. But it made a different appeal to the historical sense of its audience by incorporating the ceremonial entrance to the City of London which had stood on Fleet Street, until it presented too much of an obstacle to Victorian London's many hansom cabs and it was moved to the grounds of Theobalds Park in Hertfordshire. The hotelier Sir Hugh Wontner had long campaigned for its return to the capital and Paternoster Square provided the ideal location: commissioned by Charles II, the gateway has been attributed to Wren. Since Simpson had by now got the backing of a developer, Godfrey Bradman, the model was also on a grander scale. Described in his *Guardian* obituary as 'obsessive and idiosyncratic: a visionary but, as one partner put it, just too clever by half,' Bradman was known by a contraction of his first name – God. A workaholic, he was famous for his expansive gestures, of which the model was perhaps one.

Stuart Lipton, Bradman's partner in other projects, could see that he had been finessed. He sold his interest in Paternoster to Greycoat, a company that he had helped set up with Geoffrey

Wilson. (He went on to develop Broadgate with Bradman's Rosehaugh and make further millions from a new concept – the business park.) Wilson agreed to build Simpson's scheme, providing he could find another developer with whom to share the risk. He did so in Park Tower Realty, an American company run by George Klein, an important figure in the Jewish community and friend of the President George Bush; he was then attempting to rebuild part of Times Square in New York. 'Klein was not a player in the pantheon of big-time New York developers,' wrote Lynne B. Sagalyn in *Times Square Remade* (2023). 'He did, however, have a reputation for small, high-quality, architecturally conscious buildings, which carried significant weight with city and state officials.' The fit must have been perfect. Incredibly, Simpson's David had beaten the Arup Goliath.

The architectural historian David Watkin could hardly believe the scale of the victory at Paternoster Square, won against all the apparent odds. As he wrote in 1996:

> How amazing it is that at the end of the twentieth century, at the very heart of one of the world's great cities, a boastful monument of modernist architecture at its most brutal is about to be torn down and replaced with an $800 million development, brilliantly designed in a traditionalist architectural style that most citizens believe to be as dead as the spinning wheel.

Paternoster Square was to be reimagined as an 'urbane, gracious, bustling focus for business, shopping, and leisure north of St Paul's,' while at the same time providing a quarter more space than what had gone before. This could not have happened without the Prince of Wales – indeed it had practically been his brainchild in the first place.

When criticised for using influence, the Prince would say that he had no influence over anything. Constitutionally that may have been true but he had merely to voice an opinion for it to be splashed across many inches of newsprint and reported on the *Nine O'Clock News*. No private individual or organisation could command so much PR. He could also speak to people in high places. Besides, it was quite clear that he intended to make a difference – in other words to influence events. Speaking to a trio of editors invited to Highgrove at the end of 1987, Charles responded, according to one of those present, with 'incandescent rage' to the implication that 'he should avoid controversy by limiting himself to a life of ceremonial appearances and bland opinions.' Words burst out of him:

> 'I've had to fight every inch of my life to escape royal protocol … I've had to fight to go to university. I've had to fight to have any sort of role as Prince of Wales. You're suggesting that I go back and play polo. I wasn't trained to do that. I have been brought up to have an active role. I am determined not to be confined to cutting ribbons.

This was said 'with frightening intensity' – a reflection of the Prince's frustration at his role and his determination to be more than a national wallflower, waiting to be king. In this context, Paternoster Square not only saved the setting of St Paul's but the Prince's own equilibrium, by providing a purpose that would override the torment of being heir to the throne. The environment, architecture and inner-city regeneration were 'what the Prince [called] "the vehicle" in his campaign to create a meaningful life'.[2]

Simpson, however was new at the game. Recognising his' youth and inexperience, Greycoat and Park Tower, the new developers of the site, insisted that he should work with a more experienced masterplanner (there was a third investor, an affiliate of the

Japanese Mitsubishi Estate Company, which did not have a role in running the project). They appointed one each: Greycoat's choice was the Post-Modernist Terry Farrell, while Park Tower commissioned the American Classical architect Thomas H. Beeby. Simpson also recommended a team of like-minded architects who would be responsible for the different buildings in the scheme, the task being too much for one person. The order of battle was set out by *Architectural Design* in a book aptly titled *Paternoster Square and the New Classical Tradition* – from the numbers, it really did seem that a tradition might take root.

Building Group 1	Terry Farrell and Sidell Gibson Partnership
Building Group 2	Terry Farrell and Robert Adam
Building Group 3	Demetri Porphyrios Associates
Building Group 4	Allan Greenberg
Building Group 5	John Simpson and Partners
Building Group 6	Hammond, Beeby and Babka
Buildings in the Square	Hammond, Beeby and Babka; John Simpson and Partners
Building Group 7	Quinlan Terry
Building Group 8	Hammond, Beeby and Babka

Quinlan Terry's proposal that his building should have a section of the Lord's Prayer on the front, in reference to Paternoster, did not find favour.

The Chapter could end here. In some ways it would be happier if it did. Having set the course for the project, the Prince became an interested observer, as opposed to a protagonist, and Watkin's triumphalism in 1996 proved premature. The demand for office space crashed in the early 1990s, because of which Greycoat sold its interest in Paternoster Square for £1; Park Tower, itself in difficulties, went into liquidation leaving the project in the hands of the financiers Mitsubishi, who, not being a property developer, put the scheme on hold. Stuart Lipton saw his opportunity to return to the fray. A new scheme on the Simpson footprint was commissioned from William Whitfield; the charm of the urban square retained, along with the restored Temple Bar (although critics note that it is not attached to the buildings either side of it, as it was in Fleet Street); but the elegant and varied classicism of Simpson's brave venture was dropped. Whitfield was a man of refinement, who built a scheme that was as sympathetic to the spirit of the previous one as could be hoped. At the centre of his square is a giant column, reminiscent of the Monument but actually inspired by the columns of Inigo Jones's west front of St Paul's, which predated the Wren cathedral; there are covered colonnades on the ground floor and a repeating grid pattern above. Regularity and order are the note.

This photograph, taken during the Covid lockdown of 2020, shows Paternoster Square today, built to John Simpson's plan but by different architects, led by William Whitfield. Brick is the material that would originally have surrounded St Paul's.

What did the Prince think of it? He did not say. Public support for the monarchy slumped after Princess Diana's death on July 1, 1997. Earlier that year, a 'New Labour' government under Tony Blair had come in, with a mission to destroy tradition wherever it was found – in the House of Lords, in rural sports, in organisations such as the Boy Scouts – and rebrand Britain as a young country, under the banner of Cool Britannia. Minimalism was in, ornament out. The Prince who could do no wrong in the eyes of many newspapers was now in danger of acquiring pariah status. With his popularity rating at 20 per cent, the public relations executive Mark Bolland joined the Prince's team to close down any initiative not central to the main project, which was to rehabilitate Charles to public affection and position Camilla in such a way that she could marry him, perhaps one day becoming queen.

Much, though, had been achieved. The Whitfield scheme is immeasurably better than the Arup one. The setting of St Paul's had been saved from desecration and John Simpson's original plan was largely retained. Previously a guerrilla-like force who could do little more in public architecture than harry the RIBA establishment, the band of Classical brothers-in-arms, had, under Simpson's generalship, displayed their colours, showing that Classicism was as valid a style for office buildings as it was for country houses. Paternoster Square was noticed internationally. Park Tower exhibited the scheme in Washington DC. John Simpson was among the group who joined the Prince on Concorde to go and see it. He was also awarded the American Institute of Architects' Honor Award for Urban Design.

FOUR

HARMONY

A Vision Of Britain *and Educational Projects*

O NE NIGHT TOWARDS THE END OF HER MARRIAGE, when Princess Diana realised the enormity of what she would lose by divorce, she tried a new tactic to win back her husband. As she told Lady Colin Campbell,

> I went into his dressing room. I am wearing this fabulous eau-de-Nil silk nightdress, low-cut and slinky. I sat down on the bed beside him. He was reading one of those deadweight books by Laurens van der Post.

The mission was not a success and, as all the world knows, divorce followed. The relevance of the vignette is in showing the Prince's devotion to his mentor Laurens van der Post; through all the turbulence of those years he was able to find refuge in his works and their teaching. Van der Post died in 1996, the year that the royal couple divorced.

Like other gurus, van der Post was a complex figure and not always the person he presented in his writing. The following character sketch was written in response to a controversial but approved biography published in 2001:

> The man seems to have been quite a cad, a fantasist who continually reinvented his own heroic persona, a charming poseur of the highest order who finally became famous for simply being famous, his authenticity being largely derived from his celebrity status. He lied about many aspects of his military career, stole others' ideas and seduced women probably too numerous to mention. His famous expeditions of exploration to Malawi and the Kalahari turn out to have been about as risky as going down to the local supermarket.[1]

A close friend of the psychiatrist Carl Jung (itself no great recommendation), he was nevertheless charismatic, and Charles was not the only person to sit at his feet. Although his revelations about the natural world could be akin to fairy stories which enchanted people for reasons unconnected to objective fact, the narrative was always powerful – and who knows if they did not sometimes also contain a poetic truth? To Charles, his idea of Harmony embodied a profound wisdom.

The world of Nature, according to van der Post, was once in balance, possessed of a spiritual oneness from which mankind had become divorced by the artificial structures created by its intellect – the civilisation that was in so many ways not civilised at all. If we look, we can find the original Harmony in Nature, and to do so will bring renewal. As the embodiment of 'what is still one of the few great living symbols accessible to us – the symbol of the crown,' as van der Post wrote in a letter to the Prince, Charles could play a great role in this process. It is easy to see why this mission – the search for Harmony – should have appealed to him during the turbulent years of his first marriage.

Harmony had more than a domestic resonance, though. It would become and remain central to the Prince's view of life, the driver of all that he does. As David Cadman and Suheil Bushrui write in the introduction to his collected speeches and articles,

At the heart of everything that The Prince of Wales has tried to say for over forty years is the single theme of 'Harmony' – the overriding need for principles of balance and order as the foundation for understanding and action. Nascent in the very earliest speeches, it began to emerge more fully in the 1980s and 1990s and flourished in the first decade of the second Millennium.[2]

In a perceptive analysis in *The Spectator*, Theo Hobson describes Harmony as central to the King's 'esoteric' belief system:

Charles's creed can be summed up thus: there is divine wisdom in all human traditions, until modernity comes along and rips us away from any semblance of harmony with nature.[3]

There is little mention of Harmony in either the Hampton Court or Mansion House speeches but it is named as one of the 'Ten Principles We Can Build Upon' which Charles set out in his book *A Vision of Britain*. As yet, Harmony is not used in the holistic or full van der Postian sense, but we can see it as a staging post in the journey towards this later meaning.

In 1989 Charles had scored a royal first by making his own film, *HRH Prince of Wales: A Vision of Britain*. It was a coup for the BBC, expressed often in the Prince's own words, which, as the filmmaker Christopher Martin remembers, 'gave weight to his position because he had put his views out in the open. People respected him for it.' The documentary was followed by an exhibition and a book with

As well as master-planning Poundbury, Léon Krier was active in the New Urbanism Movement in the US, which also sought to revive the principles of the traditional city. This shows the house that Krier designed for himself at Seaside in Florida, 1985–7.

the same title. The object was to share his view of architecture with a wider public, while demonstrating that he was not simply a negative critic – he did like some recent architecture, however much the style of the RIBA establishment appalled him. So as well as an austerely Classical building by Quinlan Terry, we see Terry Farrell's colourful Henley Regatta Headquarters and John Outram's jokily Egyptian Isle of Dogs pumping station; approval is even accorded to the suave, hi-tech Modernism of the Lords Cricket Pavilion by Michael Hopkins. And across the Atlantic, Andrés Duany and Elizabeth Plater-Zyberk's Seaside in Florida, where Léon Krier had built a house for himself in the form of a temple on top of a square base, receives a particular accolade:

It is an extraordinary place – with a modern classical look. Seaside is *planned*. And it is beginning to influence architectural thinking all over the United States.

Krier would soon masterplan Poundbury for the Duchy of Cornwall.

The form of the book was not ideally suited to the message. It reminded a reviewer for the *London Review of Books* of 'the glossiest kind of Annual Report and Accounts. The company crest of three feathers decorates the end-papers'. It was decided that the words should stick closely to the script of the programme, except for the Ten Principles. As a result the text was set very large and ran over some of the illustrations. The Prince appears in the guise of Chairman, along with some of his watercolours. But if the medium was imperfect, the message rang out clearly: Modernism had been a disastrous mistake.

As a result of thirty years of experimenting with revolutionary building materials and novel ideas, burning all the rule books and purveying the theory that man is a machine, we have ended up with Frankenstein monsters, devoid of character, alien and largely unloved, except by the professors who have been concocting these horrors in their laboratories – and even they find their creations a bit hard to take after a while.

Throughout both film and book, the Prince emphasised that his opinions were his own; the book's very subtitle was 'a personal view of architecture'. But he had been pleased to discover that a lot of people agreed with him; after the *Vision of Britain* film, he received nearly 5,000 letters, 99 per cent in support. Today, it is difficult to remember what all the fuss was about; the film seems slow-moving and worthy more than contentious. Perhaps that is a sign of how far the world has moved in Charles's direction. It caused fury in some quarters at the time.

For example, the architects and critics who took part in the 'official debate' at the Victoria and Albert Museum during the exhibition that November were apoplectic. 'There they were,' wrote Elizabeth Grice in the *Sunday Times*, 'simmering with expectation at the chance to tell the Prince of Wales where to put his colonnades.' Five years of pent-up rage bubbled over. Martin Pawley of *The Guardian* called the Prince's 'approach to modern architecture a throwback to Nazi Germany,' which rejected Gropius and Mies van der Rohe in favour of traditional rows of workers' houses and the megalomaniac Classicism of Albert Speer. He was supported by Professor Colin St John ('Sandy') Wilson, architect of the new British Library.

The two men spattered the prince and his 'nostalgia-sodden image of the 18th century' for all they were worth. Full speed into the past, they called it. Vision? One of those weasel words like 'care' and 'awareness' ... They blamed him for causing good buildings to be demolished; for planning interference; for ridiculing British architects in the eyes of foreigners. They made fun of his pitched roofs and his love of chimneys. Rows of round spectacles glinted in mirth.

The President of the RIBA, Maxwell Hutchinson issued his own rebuttal in *The Prince of Wales: Right or Wrong? An Architect Replies*, published in 1989 with a foreword, inevitably, by Richard Rogers. It was not a rant but an informed account of the issues facing the future King's realm at a time of rapid change. Both sides of the argument could agree on much of the analysis and even the terms in which it was couched: 'Civility implies living in harmony with the past, the present and the future,' said Rogers in a speech quoted by Hutchinson, in words that could have been written by Charles himself. (Just as Rogers's prescription for reviving cities, when he chaired an Urban Task Force for the Blair government, would have much in common with Léon Krier's ideas for Poundbury, being informed by Rogers's Italian heritage and love of hill towns.) But the conclusion reached by Hutchinson was diametrically opposed to that of the Prince, being to promote a repurposed and newly aware Modernism. The alternative would be 'bowing and scraping our way backwards into the Carolean age [the reign of King Charles III] with a neo-classicism which ignores new technology'. Go on taking the same medicine, he seemed to be telling his readers, however little it had worked to date.

The Prince's Ten Principles – Commandments, as some jokingly called them – are remembered by one insider as having been 'dashed off by Theo Crosby – a brilliant summary, in effect, of Alberti's *On Architecture*'. They were only contentious to architects. Most people saw them as common sense. Local identities should be respected; the human scale of existing buildings should be recognised; the new should be sympathetic with the old; it should be of the same materials; architecture should help build a sense of community; the architectural hierarchy should make it immediately visible which buildings are more important than others; enclosure, decoration and works of art should be included; street signs and lights should not be allowed to litter the streetscape. In fact the reader may well find it depressing to think that these apparently obvious precepts had not been universally adopted. Everyone knew what he was driving at. On the other hand, the principles were so broadly couched that many architects and developers of whom the Prince certainly did not approve could have claimed that their work conformed to them.

There was, maybe, a degree of naivety to the Prince's stance. His favoured examples tended to be boutique buildings, architectural gems on which much creative attention had been focused. Unless cities were to stand still, ripening like apples on the bough but never getting any bigger, architects would have to address the challenge of large sites which made a commercial return. So far Paternoster Square had been one of a kind.

In *A Vision of Britain*, the Prince described Harmony as 'the playing together of the parts'. Buildings of different periods can rub along happily and create a beautiful street if they respect each other, in terms of scale and palette of materials. Contrasts are fine within reason but not the 'more extreme examples of outlandish modern design' – they would be better banished to the new towns where they would not be in competition with the old and lovely. As we have seen, Harmony was coming to have a larger meaning for the Prince, as the value which would interpenetrate and unite all his disparate interests. One of them was the Prince of Wales's Institute of Architecture, a bubbling cauldron of theories and personalities, often seemingly at odds with each other but contributing to a single goal (and to that extent partakers in Harmony) – the goal being an alternative education for architects.

The Institute, remembers Brian Hanson, who was one of the key players in it, 'was entirely an idea of HRH. He claimed that it had come to him in the bath.' It was Jules Lubbock who took this inspiration and ran with it. To Lubbock, architectural students could hardly avoid becoming Modernists because Modernism was what their long training taught them to do. This would be a theme of the book that he wrote with Mark Crinson, *Architecture: Art or Profession? Three Hundred Years of Architectural Education in Britain*, published in 1994. The authors were surprised to discover that,

The Prince of Wales talks to Mark Alexander, a 31-year-old student attending a summer school in civil architecture at Magdalen College, Oxford. Drawing was an important discipline in all the Prince's educational projects.

Designed and erected by Foundation Course students at the Prince's Institute for Architecture under John Simpson, the Pipistrelle Pavilion was intended as a bat roost. This Doric structure stands on the edge of a pond at the site of a former waterworks at Barn Elms, just south of Hammersmith Bridge and was constructed in the space of a month.

as late as 1990 when one of the major changes had been a profound and widespread public disenchantment with the modernist vision associated with the 'City of Towers', all forms of traditionalism – whether in matters of style, practice or pedagogy – were excluded from British architecture schools (and everywhere else in the world).

New movements like Post-Modernism, although apparently at odds with Modernism, might get a look in, but not Classicism, traditional methods of construction or Beaux-Arts drawing techniques. The Prince would offer an alternative through his own Institute. In 1990, the idea was trialled in the Prince of Wales's Summer School in Civil Architecture, which offered a six-week course – three weeks at Magdalen College, Oxford; two weeks at the British School at Rome; and a week at the Villa Lante in the Campagna – locations that in themselves meant living the dream. Among the cohort was Hugh Petter, now an internationally successful director of ADAM Architecture, who remembers it as 'a life-changing experience'. Until then, he had thought that he was the only person in the world with an interest in traditional architecture. Now he found himself surrounded by other students with a similar passion and a dizzying array of different teachers. As ever, the Prince wanted to stir things up. To quote Lubbock, it was at his 'suggestion that structural engineers taught side by side with highly creative architects, and that the students found themselves modelling architectural ornaments in clay and carving them in stone, as well as drawing the classical orders, learning to draw the human figure and being initiated into some of the mysteries of Platonic geometry.' There was also a fine art component taught by the artist Catherine Goodman.

That first summer school was followed by another the next year. During the Spring Lubbock parted company with the project. The irreverent and not always accurate *Private Eye* described a visit that he and Colin Amery made to discuss arrangements at Highgrove.

Much to the embarrassment of Amery, Lubbock said to the Prince that he thought it was time his contract and terms of employment were discussed as he had a wife and children to support.

The Prince excused himself from the room, and a few minutes later a minion entered, suggesting to poor Lubbock that he find his own way back to London.

According to Sir Roy Strong, something similar had happened to him, but Lubbock himself describes the story as 'completely untrue'. Amery was not there. He was not left to walk the nine miles to Kemble railway station. The Prince of Wales would never have left the room in the manner described. Certainly Lubbock had wanted a sufficiently robust contract for him to leave a tenured university post with a good pension and still support his family, and they were not able to agree terms; but he remained an active participant in the Architectural Advisory Group.

Hanson took Lubbock's place. The two summer schools paved the way for a larger, year-round enterprise – the Prince of Wales's Institute of Architecture – which opened in a pair of stucco-fronted villas in Nash's Gloucester Gate, in London's Regent's Park. It offered an expanded version of the summer school programme as a foundation course. As Hanson recalls,

> We felt that the first year of architecture school was often where the most 'damage' was done: where students were encouraged to forget everything they knew, and adopt instead a 'new' outlook that turned its back on tried and tested solutions. Because of this I believe that some of the students who were able to vault into Year 2 of a degree on the back of our course were better able to stand up to the 'brainwashing' endemic to other schools.

Twelve hours were spent in observational drawing each week.

Both the summer schools and the foundation course emphasised making. Petter, no longer a student but a part-time tutor, helped to run an Arts and Crafts programme.

Everyone learnt to see, to draw and to make things – learning by doing. Craftsmen like the stone carver Dick Reid would appear. Students would be taken to Surrey to be shown Arts and Crafts country houses by the specialist in the period Roderick Gradidge, looking like a pirate with his hair in a pigtail and a Cumbrian kilt lower down, or to make a green-oak building in the garden of the watercolour genius, Alexander Creswell – they cut all the timber out of fallen oak trees and made every joint by hand. It's still there and used as a shed.

Every year something different was created. An information kiosk made for the makers in the Jewellery Quarter in Birmingham is now a locally listed building. During the summer schools, two timber shelters were constructed under the inspiration of Imre Makovecz, a Hungarian architect who, during the years of

Led by the architect Hugh Petter (in the red jersey in the back row), a team of students from the Prince's Institute for Architecture designed a barn at the home of another of the Institute's teachers, the painter Alexander Creswell, in Surrey in 1996. There were different hands-on projects every year, which provided students with a level of practical experience they would not have obtained at a conventional architectural school.

Communism, had developed what Jonathan Glancey's *Guardian* obituary called a 'compelling, idiosyncratic and organic style, borrowing from nature' and re-interpreting the ideas of Rudolf Steiner, Frank Lloyd Wright, Antoni Gaudí and his fellow-countryman Ödön Lechner. ('Makovecz's buildings represent beacons of sanity in a maelström of materialism and mediocrity,' Charles would write in his foreword to a book about the architect written by Anthony Tischhauser in 2001. 'They stand out bravely as symbols of faith, of proportion and, above all, of true humanity. Every detail of them, within and without, lifts the spirit and gladdens the heart.') One of the shelters, erected with the assistance of the master's studio, survived for 25 years. John Simpson directed the erection of a wooden, proto-Doric structure on the site on the wetlands of Barnes; intended as a bat roost, it was called the Pipistrelle Pavilion.

These fun projects took the students through the various stages of architecture: conceiving an idea, drawing it, working with the client to develop a brief, deciding how to build the project, and clambering over scaffolding in the wind and rain while it was under construction. It was an approach that could help students who might otherwise have been overlooked – for example, a builder with no formal qualifications to his name who had therefore been denied access to higher education: 'He went straight into the secondary year of an undergraduate degree at De Montfort and came out 2 years later with first class honours.' The idea was that students would become 'apostles' of a different approach to architecture, which they would spread by their example through the profession. Strangely, graduates from the Institute who went on to architecture school were well received because their accomplishments made them more interesting than the usual run of school leavers.

To the foundation course was added a graduate course, joined by Ben Pentreath in 1995 after a degree in the History of Art at Edinburgh University. Pentreath was one of many students to whom the Institute gave an alternative entry into architecture. 'It was fantastic but crazy – completely chaotic. Nostalgia was mixed with zaniness.' By then a diploma course, equivalent to the Part 2 of an architecture school, had been added to the foundation and graduate courses, in the hope of its being validated by the RIBA so that students could use their diploma towards an eventual degree and qualification to practise.

Pentreath is not alone in his affectionate memory of the chaos, a word that is not necessarily pejorative. The most creative art and architecture schools often do bring people of strong passions and conflicting ideas into proximity – with sometimes explosive results. To students, the drama can be intoxicating. They can take from the offering what they will, knowing that they will themselves soon have moved on to other things. Even so, not all the students liked it. Coming from Poland, where the teaching of architecture was still as conservative and methodical as it had been under the recently disbanded Communist regime, Joanna Wachowiak, now a director of John Simpson Architects, found the lack of system frustrating and inefficient. Nor did it always appeal to members of staff. Corporations provide their executives with management training to create a temperate work environment – hardly stimulating but less stressful for people who thrive on order and calm. Given that the Prince finds the conventional, profit-driven business outlook to be utterly alien to him, he has probably never gone on a management course in his life. This showed in the structure of the organisation. It was difficult for the director to set a clear course when teachers beneath him could always promote their own special interests by going direct to The Boss, as the Prince was generally known. Everyone had Bernie the butler's number at Highgrove and would be put through. As an enthusiast, the Prince might take fire at the idea and adopt it – meaning that the director had been outflanked. Directors, unsurprisingly perhaps, kept changing. (Colin Amery joked that it should be renamed the Institute of Directors.) Alan Powers, who became the Institute's Librarian thinks this contributed to – or was a reflection of – the Institute's 'weird difficulty in deciding what it was'. But to both him and the student body, shielded from the turmoil at the top, it was a 'fantastic experience'. It was also very well funded, with generous scholarships, an extraordinary array of tutors, sometimes flown in at great expense, and subsidised free trips to New York and Italy for short architecture courses. What was not to like about that?

In popular mythology, the Institute was a Classical project, but the brief was really much wider. While the Classicists John Simpson and Demetri Porphyrios taught there, so did New Urbanists like Léon Krier and Andrés Duany. As well as Nick Wates and John Thompson, who taught Community Architecture, and the craftsman-architect Ben Tindall, the students also encountered Islamic architects such as Abdel-Wahed El-Wakil, and Keith Critchlow, an expert in the sacred geometry of Islam. Then came the artists, such as Jane Dowling, Norman Blamey and Catherine Goodman. The idea was that hand skills and habits of hard work were as important in the foundation course as untrammelled imagination, as cultivated in conventional schools. Life drawing classes were a regular evening fixture, while drawing of the orders was taught by Julian Bicknell. Lectures might be delivered by members of the Temenos Academy, a forum for 'spirituality in the arts conducted by redoubtable poet Kathleen Raine.'

Visiting from Berkeley and with the sound of Mahler, played at high volume, emanating from his studio, the empirical philosopher-architect Christopher Alexander was a prominent

The future Charles III visits the holy sites of Uzbekistan in 1996, in company with the champion of sacred geometry, Keith Critchlow, an influential figure in the Prince's educational projects. With them is the artist Emma Sargent.

figure – to the exasperation of colleagues. Author of *A Pattern Language*, which analysed the patterns that are most conducive to human feelings of *Gemütlichkeit*, he advocated 'not-separateness', described by a follower as meaning to 'evolve and shape what you're making so that it is connected to everything else it can possibly connect to'. Such ideas appealed to Charles, who would sometimes call himself a Neo-Platonist (a school of philosophy that saw a universal oneness in everything). So the Classical architecture, which students were taught to draw, and the Arts and Crafts structures, which they built from trees they had cut down themselves, shared a common root, both being derived from Nature (the very words used to describe the elements of a Classical column show how closely the Ancients lived with the natural world – echinus, for example, means hedgehog). Forget the surface chaos; beneath it all, Harmony held sway.

On the face of it, Harmony may not always seem to have been the presiding virtue of Charles's educational endeavours, but to some extent, they were an expression of his philosophy in which the word is used in a special sense. Apparent opposites could be made to exist within the same building. While the eternal rules of Classicism and the omnipresent geometrical patterns of Nature suggest the existence of universal truths, Charles was equally passionate about difference. As he wrote in the introduction to a book of the architect Mark Hoare's watercolours, after the Institute had morphed into a Foundation, the destruction of

> this most precious and fragile diversity ... suck[ed] out the character, charm and spiritual meaning from every pore of our human experience. This book then is a heartfelt cry for greater sensitivity to place and encompasses everything that my Foundation stands for. The living tradition of buildings and cultural continuity, a celebration of difference within this

living universal tradition and the recognition of connections between painting, architecture, landscape, agriculture and the spiritual journey itself.[4]

It was, to say the least, a challenge for Brian Hanson and the panoply of directors to orchestrate the Institute's many voices and make sense of the Prince's 'complex vision'. Some of the lecturers could not stand each other. To use a political metaphor of the time, it was a big tent. Rupert Sheldrake, the biologist who champions morphic resonance, the memory innate in Nature; the Spanish architect and engineer Santiago Calatrava; even Norman Foster – all could come in. When Richard John, a protégé of David Watkin, attempted to impose a more strictly Classical identity on the amorphous – if not anarchic – Institute, he only lasted nine months. Occasionally the Prince himself would drop in unannounced, until a journalist reported a question he asked, with the object of making him appear somewhat naïve. Charles's staff ensured that impromptu visits were reduced.

In 1994, Hanson was asked to extend the reach of the Institute by designing a practical complement to its educational programme. The Prince expressed the hope that overseas summer schools

would develop into something rather like a task force, which included some of the best *practitioners* who could be understudied and assisted by 'apprentices'. I am sure far more would be learnt from a 'master' than any other way – *despite* the modern trend against such an approach.[5]

It would not only be the students who stood to benefit, but the intense focus on the problems of a historic town or city – albeit for only three or four weeks – could be a boon to places that were struggling to find a way forward. The Appendix (see pp. 221-22) shows where the ten Urban Task Forces that were held during the programme's four years of operation were focused. Projecting the Prince's ideas onto the international stage, they were one of his most successful initiatives.

Hanson describes how they worked:

We responded to invitations, whether from Institutions (eg. St Petersburg Academy of Arts), Mayors (eg. Caprarola), Senior Planning Officers (eg. Potsdam), or Prime Ministers (Rafic al-Hariri for Beirut/Sidon). We would then plan a programme lasting between 2 and 6 weeks, recruit an international body of students, assign tutors (such as Maurice Culot, Lucien Steil, Samir Younés), and invite selected alumni back to be Teaching Assistants. The host city (supported in many cases by local companies) would provide studio and accommodation space, and food, and they would select a site of pressing interest for the students to work on. In the case of Caprarola this would involve a series of interventions along the whole length of the city, in other cases (such as Potsdam) it would be interventions at one or two local sites. The whole high-pressure exercise would culminate in a public exhibition of student proposals in a central venue, and a personal visit by The Prince of Wales. Over the years of our Task Force work we also held conferences sponsored by local newspapers and discussions attended by senior government figures. We generated a great deal of local coverage of our activities, and subsequently published a sponsored book of our conclusions, both of which drew attention to specific local urban challenges and ways in which traditional urban approaches might address them.

The media attention given to visits by the Prince of Wales ensured that the efforts of each Urban Task Force were noticed locally. There could be concrete results. At Potsdam, for example, described by the Prince as a 'picturesque, pastoral dream', which fulfilled the human longing for a relationship with the world our species inhabits 'through a balance between architecture and the natural world,' the Task Force boosted local efforts to reconstruct the central Stadtschloss, destroyed during the last days of the Second World War and cleared in the 1960s. The Stadtschloss was rebuilt in 2010–13.

But at Gloucester Gate the drama continued. At the end of 1996 all 15 members of the Institute's governing Council stood down: pressure was said to have been applied by Mark Bolland, the 31-year-old marketing executive who had become Charles's new Deputy Private Secretary. There was also a new director, the archaeologist Richard Hodges, charged with moving the Institute from its Nash terrace to somewhere grungier. Stylistic issues, he announced, were not of interest – the Institute was not a champion of Classicism. If the object was to build a better relationship with the RIBA, as the body which had to approve the diploma course, it failed. When Ben Pentreath was halfway through his year on the graduate course, word came that the diploma course would not be accredited, dashing the hope that the Institute would become a fully fledged alternative choice for future architects. Supposedly, the RIBA took this decision on the grounds that no director lasted more than a year, although a member of the board told Lubbock that it was wholly to do with the style being taught.

Hardly had the Institute regained its equilibrium before it was blown down for good by the hurricane surrounding the death of Princess Diana on August 31, 1997. Britain was swept by a tsunami of grief, expressed in an ever-growing bow wave of flowers left by members of the public at the gates of Kensington Palace.

Already cast as the villains in Diana's unhappy story, the Royal Family was condemned for an insufficient display of anguish. With the efficiency with which the Royal Family traditionally acts to protect itself, a rescue mission was launched. Bolland was tasked with terminating what were deemed to be loony or potentially controversial projects. The Prince's architectural agenda was hated by Modernists and easy to misrepresent in the media as being backward-looking, elitist or bonkers. So the Institute had to go. The doors closed in 1998. The Urban Task Force programme went down with the ship.

This reflects a paradox of the British monarchy, the construct within which Charles has spent his life and which, even as King, it is beyond him to reform. Having given him a voice by virtue of his position, the institution is then intent on muffling the sound. As one insider puts it,

> he exists within a machine that is beautifully engineered to suck out all the energy from him. Setting up initiatives to do good and bring people together are fine as long as they don't go too far. If they do, the machine swings into action to ensure the effort is dissipated.

This may be only one view but seems to explain the demise of the Institute, which had not been a failure; on the contrary it had been a success that showed every prospect of creating a different architectural tradition – 'the only radically alternative, stand-alone teaching institution attempted so far in Britain' since the beginning of the 20th century. To Ben Pentreath its end raises an interesting question:

> What if it hadn't closed down in 1998? I think the impact now from all the people that had passed through would be

incredible. There is now a much smaller pool of talent because of that sad ending. The graduate course was an incredible crucible – quite mad but profound.

Unpredictable to the end, the Institute's last director was Adrian Gale, a Modernist, lately retired from being head of Plymouth School of Architecture: he had at one point worked in Mies van der Rohe's office.

The only parts of the Institute to survive were the department of Visual Islamic and Traditional Arts (VITA), renamed the School of Traditional Arts, and the drawing course, reinvented as the Royal Drawing School: they were repackaged as the Prince's Foundation and moved to a new building in earthy but up-and-coming Shoreditch. Not only does Charles have a deep passion for Islamic art and figure drawing (deeper than is often realised, in the case of Islamic art), but they were judged to be safe spaces for him to move in. That assessment proved correct; they were hardly noticed by the press.

The Prince's Foundation lives on as the King's Foundation, but – in the manner of Chairman Mao's China – has been in a state of perpetual revolution since its inception. Nevertheless it has kept going and, as will be seen in the final chapter, constitutes a palpable legacy from Charles's years as Prince of Wales. A management consultant might not approve of every aspect of its structure or practice, but there is no shortage of ideas.

With the closure of the Institute, Harmony would be preached from other pulpits – for example, in a book of that name published by Charles with Tony Juniper and Ian Skelly in 2010. *Harmony* includes a long section on sacred geometry, which bears witness to the Prince's deep knowledge of architecture, gleaned in part from his travels: the same recurring themes can be found in 'the great shrine to the Lord Buddha at Borobudur in Indonesia or the Parthenon 6,000 miles away in Greece, or one of the great Gothic cathedrals of Northern Europe'. But this is not an architectural manifesto; the vision is broader. The 'lines and shapes of architecture' are but one aspect of the 'natural order and rhythm of things', also to be found in 'the processes involved in agriculture, and certainly in the natural world as a whole'. To paraphrase Christopher Alexander's philosophy, everything is connected to everything else. The place where Charles could most fully demonstrate this idea was his own home, garden and Duchy Farm at Highgrove.

FIVE

COUNTRYSIDE

The Idyll of Highgrove

S INCE BECOMING KING, CHARLES III HAS PLANTED many trees. This is not a reflection of the royal obligation to spade in commemorative trees on ceremonial occasions, but the result of a personal, almost obsessive passion. If his staff lose track of him around Windsor Castle, they joke that he is probably tree-planting – and as often as not, that is exactly what he is doing. It goes back a long way. In 1992, he spoke of his joy of planting trees at Highgrove in a television programme on royal gardens presented by Sir Roy Strong. When still a novice at gardening, he would put them too close together, forgetting how tall they would grow; but the fact that they had been dug in by his own labour made him reluctant to take them down.

According to Robert Hardman's *Charles III: The Inside Story*, he is proving to be an even more active Ranger of Windsor Great Park than his father. This is not only because of his love of detail; he loves the countryside too. This in turn permeates his other passions and activities, including architecture.

If Queen Elizabeth II had not been head of state, she might have been happy as a country gentlewoman, devoted to her horses, her dogs and her family – possibly in that order. She gave her eldest son a country childhood. We glimpse him in the press as a small boy among the daffodils of Royal Lodge, Windsor, or on holiday at Balmoral, kilted and leading a calf. At 13 Prince Charles is bravely marching into Gordonstoun, as rigorously outdoors a school as it was possible to find – it was there that he developed an appetite for taking long country hikes, perhaps to escape the place; at Sandringham, he heaps logs on bonfires and rides out with Princess Anne. Polo and hunting were pursued passionately, despite many falls – a day in the saddle might be followed by an evening of romance with one of the girls he had seen while he was out. As soon as he acquired Highgrove, at the age of 31, calmer passions came into play. Working with the Marchioness of Salisbury, called by the *New York Times* the High Priestess of

Highgrove House outside Tetbury, built in the 1790s, was probably designed by the Gloucestershire architect Anthony Keck. By the time it was acquired by the Duchy of Cornwall for Prince Charles, in 1980, it had been much changed from this print of 1825.

Gardening, he flattened the old garden and planned a new one. At Cranborne Manor in Dorset and Hatfield House in Hertfordshire, Lady Salisbury – Mollie as her friends knew her – sought to capture 'the manner and character' (her words) of the early 17th-century gardens designed by the Tradescants, father and son, while applying to them her own poetic eye. This was also the spirit of Highgrove, where the Prince hoped that his garden would evoke the order of an earlier age, combined with the beauty of Nature. Its evolution over 40 years will be described in the next chapter. Here it is enough to say that the Prince extended the realm of beauty to include the wider estate, which surrounded his home.

Strictly speaking, Highgrove was not an estate, which generally means a landholding of thousands of acres, including many tenanted farms. Under 350 acres went with the house – a hand-kerchief in comparison to the Duchy of Cornwall's entire estate of 130,000 acres. (As King, Charles no longer possesses even those 350, having decided in 2020 not to renew the lease from the Duchy which would soon be in his son William's hands, as next Duke of Cornwall, meaning that he would have to pay rent.) It had never been more than a farm and quite a small farm, by commercial standards, at that; nor had it been a royal possession until the Duchy bought it. And yet almost immediately it assumed enormous personal significance. By 1993, when he and Charles Clover published *Highgrove: Portrait of an Estate*, the Prince would write:

I have put my heart and soul into Highgrove … All the things I have tried to do in this small corner of Gloucestershire have been the physical expression of a personal philosophy. When I was younger I recall the nascent stirrings of such a philosophy; I felt a strong attachment to the soil of those places I loved best – Balmoral, in Scotland, and Sandringham, in Norfolk. As far as I was concerned, every tree, every hedgerow, every wet place, every mountain and river had a special, almost sacred, character of its own.

The land was deeply important to him. Having already made his views on agriculture known through his speeches, he immediately converted the farming operation to the organic system. This improved the soil, encouraged more worms to live in it, provided a well-stocked larder of bugs for wildlife to thrive on, and turned a modest profit (which might not have been possible if the Duchy had not owned the land, meaning that the Prince could use it rent free). In the Picturesque tradition, he also made

Holding a shepherd's crook as a walking stick, Prince Charles walks the Duchy Home Farm at Highgrove with his elder son, Prince William, the present Prince of Wales. At under 350 acres, the farm became a showcase for organic agriculture.

it part of a visual unity with the house. Duchy Home Farm was in effect his park, of a piece with the garden. The Prince farmed beauty and Nature as well as animals and oats.

The effect was captured by Caroline Boucher when she visited for *The Observer* in 2003.

> Ruby and Annabel, two gorgeous Tamworth sows, are sunning themselves outside their hut. In the distance, a rare Welsh Black cow sits on the grass, her coat so shiny it looks as if it has been washed and conditioned. Behind her, the top two floors of one of Britain's most famous privately owned country houses can be seen just above the oak trees ... Duchy Home is truly a model farm, one that you see only in children's books or on the Disney screen: poker-straight fences, immaculately painted farm buildings, glossy animals, chickens pecking round the swept yard and not a discarded piece of rusting machinery in sight.

A sign at the beginning of the drive into Highgrove reads: 'Beware. You are entering an old-fashioned establishment.' This being the Prince of Wales's project, the seriousness of the undertaking – the production of food being so important for Nature, human health and carbon emissions – did not entirely crowd out charm.

As ever, the Prince's vision was, in a favourite word, holistic: not only was the farm one with the garden but Charles's love of the land is expressed in two buildings that he commissioned: the Orchard Room and the Sanctuary. Both, in the Arts and Crafts manner, look as though they have grown out of the soil on which they stand, the walls of the Sanctuary being literally built of it. Because the whole aim of his philosophy is to re-establish the Harmony that should exist between humanity and Nature, they also exhibit high levels of craftsmanship; hand work is not only beautiful of itself but gives meaning to the life of the person practising the skill.

During the 1990s, Charles found it increasingly difficult to spend the time he would have liked at Highgrove. While his mother – now past the State retirement age – remained energetic, it was clear that more of the burden of monarchy would be shared with her eldest son, if only to give him a sense of purpose as he waited in the wings. This would mean more travel and official engagements, and even greater exposure to the press than he already got. He could not bear the thought of spending the rest of his work time in London, only to visit his Gloucestershire refuge for the occasional weekend. So in a departure from royal precedent, he made it clear that Highgrove would become his principal base of operations rather than St James's Palace or Clarence House. People who wanted to see him would have to make the journey there.

And make the journey they did – in droves. His charities, the business initiatives he supported, the different branches of the armed services – he entertained them all, often to lunch or dinner in a marquee, or an evening reception in the garden, and he would work the room assiduously, with words for every single guest to make him or her feel special. On top of that, 200 groups were coming to visit the garden. What happened, though, if it rained? Marquees are not in every way ideal for catering but at Highgrove they became a semi-permanent fixture. To this problem the Prince had an innovative solution. He would build a structure, appropriate to its garden setting, where both large receptions and smaller lunches could take place. The choice of architect fell on the Suffolk-based Charles Morris, whom the Prince had met when visiting Gervase Jackson-Stops, the architectural advisor to the National Trust, at The Menagerie in Northamptonshire. The Menagerie had been built in the 1730s to keep its aristocratic

On acquiring Highgrove, Prince Charles quickly began developing a garden; this photograph shows the famous Thyme Walk. The house itself also became increasingly engulfed in vegetation.

owner's exotic animals and Jackson-Stops was restoring it, along with the Rococo plasterwork inside, to become a house; Morris had just added a portico to the south side. After some months, a call came from Sandringham requesting Morris's presence there the next day, with photographs of his work. Photographs were found, with some difficulty, and Morris set off to meet the Duchy of Cornwall's agent, Jimmy James. 'I felt I had to say to him that I wasn't a qualified architect but a surveyor, mostly working on estate management. To which Jimmy threw himself on the carpet, raised his hands and said "Praise be to God!"' They had found it difficult to identify a qualified architect with the right sensibility. After a short meeting with the Prince, he was given the brief by James and the Prince's indispensable valet Michael Fawcett. As yet there had been no talk of style or budget.

It was now late November 1996 and Morris finished the drawings on Boxing Day. They were soon shown to the Prince. 'I was impressed by how quickly he understood the drawings. In no time at all he looked at me and said, "Now, you're a very clever architect." And we were away.' One of Morris's challenges had been to produce a building that would serve such a variety of different audiences. As Michael Hall wrote in *Country Life*, it had to 'seem welcoming to an old lady in stout brogues who has just tramped round the garden in the rain as well as a millionaire in evening dress attending a fund-raising dinner.' Another challenge was the site – near the Georgian formality of Highgrove House, the vernacular barns of the Home Farm and the Prince of Wales's magnificent garden, and looking out over a glorious Cotswold landscape. A location was found on an old orchard, which gave it the name of the Orchard Room; care was taken that it was easily accessible on the garden site but did not obtrude too much into the park. The form of the building was relatively simple, consisting principally of an anteroom on the west front and a large space – the Orchard Room itself – divided into three bays by traverse vaults, which help with the acoustics. On the outside these bays are expressed by three gables, suggestive of turn-of-the-20th-century Arts and Crafts architecture (repeating gables, derived from Elizabethan buildings, became a hallmark of Philip Webb). There was a shop facing the house, and kitchens and lavatories towards the farm on the north.

The genius of the building is that it appears to be equally comfortable as a companion to Highgrove as it is to the farm. This was achieved by a seemingly merry (in truth, carefully considered) stylistic insouciance, which combines a screen of tubby columns, clearly inspired by the Market Hall at nearby Tetbury, with less formal elements, such as the rubblestone bases on which they stand or an enclosing dry stone wall. The Prince 'loved my fat columns,' Morris remembers. Great attention was paid to the materials. Outside, the stone face was cut back after insertion to make the joint with the render dead flush. Living in the Cotswolds around Cirencester, you've just got stone – a lovely chalky white which sets it off completely. Hence the render on the face of the gables.

Internally, the roof of the Orchard Room is supported on unmoulded columns, divided into bands of light and dark stone. It is Morris's theory that nobody can feel lonely if there's a column.

> If you got to a party on your own and know nobody you can feel very alone. But if you have a column to stand by or lean against, you are not alone. You can calmly survey the room. Prince Charles just got it before I told him.

Apple branches drawn by Ben Pentreath twine in a band of plasterwork around the ceiling in a reference to the old orchard. Blazing logs crackle in the fireplace on chilly days; to avoid the need for a chimney, this is contained in a tall stove such as one might find in Central Europe or Scandinavia. The effect is rustic Baroque.

A limed-oak door, leading from the anteroom to the Orchard Room, required particular thought. How should it be detailed? As Michael Hall describes, 'Feeling that traditional raised and fielded panelling … would be too smart for such a building, and vernacular bead-and-butt was too humble, Mr Morris designed a square pattern of reeding which is tactile and catches the light in a subtle way.' Light was important for the Prince as well as Morris. As the latter recalls:

> Working with HRH was an absolute delight. He was so positive about things. Before we even started building he'd gone up to Orkney and he'd visited Melsetter on Hoy [an Arts and Crafts country house by W.R. Lethaby], where he

wrote me a lovely letter about how the light played and the contrast of light and dark. He was immensely heartened because he felt quite certain that my building would have some of that spirit in it. He is very sensitive with the spirit of a building and the sense of a place. I see it as an architect's role to know about these things. Clients don't normally; they just appreciate the end result.

To try out the iron chandeliers for the Orchard Room, the Prince had a prototype rigged up in the ballroom at Sandringham. 'He liked it very much but said the arms were a tiny bit too thin. And he was absolutely right.' When finished, the Orchard Room was decorated with the kilims and textiles that the Prince bought on

Inside the Orchard Room at Highgrove, logs can blaze on the hearth of a stove-like fireplace, which removes the need for a chimney. Apple branches twine in a band of plasterwork around the ceiling.

his travels around the world, during which potential vendors from the bazaar would be sourced by the ubiquitous Michael Fawcett and display their wares to the Prince in the privacy of the rooms where he was staying; one of the restrictions of royal life was that Charles could not indulge in a public shopping expedition.

As Morris was finishing the Orchard Room, he was asked to contribute to a small building in the grounds of Highgrove which more fully expresses the King's spirituality than anything else that he has created. This is the Sanctuary. When the King returns to Highgrove, the first thing he will do is to go there in search of spiritual solace through calm contemplation: the Sanctuary is the emblem of the Harmony that he forever seeks but all too often finds lacking in human affairs. To save him from having to find a key to this sacred space, it has four knobs which must be turned in a secret way for the door to open; intruders fumbling for the right combination would be spotted on camera before they could enter. Nobody apart from the King and his closest friends and family is allowed in.

Previously, the Prince had obtained a design from Keith Critchlow, an artist who had written widely on sacred geometry in books such as *Order in Space*, *Islamic Patterns*, *Time Stands Still* and *The Hidden Geometry of Flowers*. As professor of Islamic Art at the Royal College of Art, he had founded the Visual Islamic and Traditional Arts (VITA) department in 1984, which moved to the Prince of Wales's Institute of Architecture eight years later. Morris was reluctant to work on someone else's project but the Prince continued to press for his help. Critchlow was no more anxious to collaborate than Morris and he withdrew from the process. Morris produced a design that he describes as English Orthodox in spirit: a quatrefoil with a barrel vault. 'The Prince just loved it.' Months later, Morris came across a book by Lethaby that cited William of Malmesbury's account of a church built by

Alfred the Great on the Somerset Levels. 'It described almost exactly what I'd done. It was uncanny.'

At most, six people can get into the Sanctuary at the same time. The scale recalls the verse in Matthew, chapter 18: 'For where two or three are gathered together in my name, there am I in the midst of them.' The approach is subtly mediated so that visitors are mentally prepared to enter an important space before they reach it. Two columns stand in front of the doorway, to indicate that architecture of some kind lies within. The apron of ground in front of the entrance is subtly sunk, again to prepare the mind for a transition. When Morris suggested that the materials from which the Sanctuary is made should be as natural as possible, the King loved the idea. Consequently the walls are made from Cotswold stone and clay lump (unfired brick), comprising soil from the farm with added chalk. Thirty-seven different moulds were needed to make the building's various shapes.

> They need six weeks to dry, in the air but under cover so they don't get wet. We had planned to use the lambing sheds, but lambing was late so they were in use. We used the drive instead but there was torrential rain and the whole lot went to mud. And he was there for the weekend but he didn't even worry about it. It is incredibly sustainable because it doesn't need cooking. Once it is in the building you need to render it and it is the same mix but with less cut straw in it. It isn't prone to return to mud because it casts rain and you need a good eave.

The floor is composed from a mixture of sand and lime, on top of a tar base – there is no plastic damp-proof course. Sweet chestnut was chosen for the roof, being resistant to woodworm. On the windows, the draft seals are leather.

The construction of the Sanctuary was supervised by Mark

Charles III loses no opportunity to reconnect with the world of Nature, believing that its patterns and proportions should be embodied in that of architecture. Here he is seen feeding chickens at Highgrove.

Hoare, a young alumnus of the Institute, then working in Charles Morris's office. (The Institute 'completely changed my life,' Hoare remembers; he had previously read Classics at Oxford.) He found that Charles was

> passionate about the use of local materials and the feeling of a building having grown out of the place. He wanted a more organic architecture, deeply rooted in the spot it was built. Organic farming and The Boss's views on architecture are close bedfellows.

The stained-glass artist John Napper provided windows on a theme of Nature which are dedicated to the poet Ted Hughes. An uncut stone, marked only with bands to match the courses of stone on the Sanctuary's internal columns, provides an altar-like focus. Over time, the space has acquired pairs of Orkney chairs as well as many icons in the Russian Orthodox tradition. The King's friend, the Right Revd Richard Chartres, Bishop of London, whose bust can be seen in the garden, conducted the opening ceremony.

Here, in the midst of the garden which has been an ongoing process of creation since the 1980s, is the still centre of the King's life.

SIX

ARCADIA

The Garden at Highgrove

I N 1992, SIR ROY STRONG TOOK A TELEVISION CREW to Highgrove, making part of a series on royal parks and gardens. The episode begins with an account of gardening in Elizabeth II's reign – a story of post-war austerity, when gardens, even royal ones, were being reduced and simplified, due to soaring costs and a lack of gardeners. In response to social change, all the Queen's gardens were opened to the public in some way. By contrast to the retrenchment of his parent's generation, the Prince of Wales had created the 'most important garden laid out in the 1980s'. This was in tune with the times. The Thatcher decade saw a revival of the country house, as owners – no longer so punitively taxed as they had been – rediscovered their confidence. Rather than convenient, modern houses near a golf course and within easy commuting distance of London, the advertising pages of *Country Life*, now full of sporting estates in counties like Gloucestershire, focused on country houses with pediments and columns. Gardens part of the dream. Indeed, they were often the dreamiest element, being nostalgic in form and romantically planted – a revival of the Arts and Crafts belonging to country houses like Rodmarton and Hidcote, the latter being a favourite of Prince Charles.

Although the Highgrove garden was relatively young, many hands had already been at work on it. Two of them belonged to Charles himself, since it was clear that he loved the physical activity of gardening as well as the aesthetics. He would point to a bench, saying 'I painted that seat, it was an awful brown colour.' He got down on his knees to plant the famous thyme walk. Hedgelaying held no terrors for him: not only did he become adept at it but would happily return from a morning's work with his forearms cut to pieces by thorns. At first, the Prince had hoped to find an advisor in Lanning Roper, the American doyen of garden designers, who had taken part in the D-Day landings and won the US Gold Star medal before discovering his vocation in horticulture, but he was already too ill from cancer before his death in 1983. Instead it was Vernon Russell-Smith who joined Charles in digging the holes in which the trees of the lime avenue were planted – 'you actually garden with the prince.' Russell-Smith was Felix Kelly's partner; in a later age he might have become his husband, but at that distant date, they were supposed only to be neighbours occupying adjacent flats in a building in Prince's Gate. (Kelly would 'roar up in a fast car with this blonde woman on his arm as a disguise,' a friend told a journalist for the *New Zealand Herald*. 'But they knew of course.') A letter from Charles to Russell-Smith that found its way into the salerooms is dated February 16, 1986 and describes the recuperative effects that gardening will have after a flight back from Texas.

There are one or two things I would like advice on. One is an idea I have been considering for the 'Savill' garden bit, which would involve creating a landscaped bank of soil against the low wall, which runs round the outside of the Savill garden, so that one could plant evergreen shrubs etc on the top of it in order to create a natural screen from the back drive. At present there are hurdles along the wall to act as a screen, but they rot so quickly. We have masses of spare soil from excavations at the new home farm – and the machinery to spread it about.

The Savill garden was so called from the plants transported from the Savill Garden at Windsor. Clearly the Prince was thinking in detail about its development.

In Roy Strong's television programme, Charles reveals his debt to his grandmother, whose gardens he 'loved'. He also took inspiration from the Marchioness of Salisbury, who encouraged him not only to create the garden at Highgrove but may have led him to talk to his plants – an apparent eccentricity with which satirists have made hay ever since. 'Don't all gardeners do that?' Lady Salisbury is supposed to have said. (Mockers may be disquieted by recent research indicating that trees can indeed communicate with each other through mycorrhizal networks underground, not that human speech is quite the same thing.) Like Charles, 'Mollie' was a committed organic gardener who banished pesticides and artificial fertilisers from her realm. That realm was extensive, comprising first Cranborne Manor in Dorset and then, after her husband inherited from his father, Hatfield House in Hertfordshire, along with another garden in Provence. Lady Salisbury helped Charles design the walled vegetable garden, restraining his love of elaborate knots and interlacing patterns out of box in the 'Old English' manner; they would be too difficult for the gardeners to tend properly. The Prince concurred, joking that otherwise he would have to employ a one-legged gardener to hop from bed to bed. Not everything in the garden was edible. Tunnels were made out of scented sweet pea, because they were more aesthetically

The wildflower meadow was planted with a mix of seed from 32 species in 1982 and sown with the help of the entomologist and botanist Dr Miriam Rothschild. Conscious of the precipitous decline of wildflower meadows after the Second World War, the Prince would become an active patron of the wildflower charity Plantlife after its foundation in 1989.

pleasing than runner beans. The billowing fruit trees which look like mounds of ice cream in spring would not have been allowed in a Victorian vegetable garden, since they shade out some of the plants.

When he wrote *Royal Gardens*, the book of the series, Sir Roy got into trouble with one of the courtiers who vetted the draft, for suggesting that potagers – decorative vegetable gardens – were the height of fashion at the time Charles's had been made. The Prince of Wales does not follow fashion, he was told. And yet the Prince did. As the television programme makes clear, the Prince was, in 1992, still learning the ropes of gardening. He leant heavily on his Gloucestershire neighbour Rosemary Verey, whose four-acre garden at Barnsley House, begun when she was in her 40s, loosely reflected, as Penelope Hobhouse wrote in an obituary, 'the 17th-century architecture of the property, a former rectory belonging to her husband's family. On it she focused her sharp mind, knowledge of garden history, and familiarity with plants – combined with an extraordinary colour sense.' Verey helped with the cottage garden. Sir Roy's contribution was to plan and clip the topiary, some of it from pre-existing yews which would grow again in no time however vigorously they were cut back. Swags were the note, to begin with. Pediments over doorways and bobbles and animals on top of the hedges would come later, once the topiarist had more material to sculpt. Since the 1970s, Sir Roy had been developing his own garden at The Laskett in Herefordshire, a sort of mini-Versailles that, through the different garden areas and follies, told the story of his life, together with that of his co-gardener and wife, the set designer Julia Trevelyan Oman. The Laskett was the largest formal garden to be created in the second half of the 20th century. Topiary appealed to the Prince, with his taste for whimsy and embellishment.

So by 1992 the plateau of bare earth had been transformed

into a series of enclosed rooms – a rose garden, planted with old-fashioned roses; a cottage flower garden; and a large formal garden enclosed by hedges. To the east was a woodland which was developed into an arboretum; the productive walled kitchen garden was given a new look in the style of Rosemary Verey's 'potager'. The ambition was impressive; so was the speed at which it had all been created. Only one feature could be called pioneering and that was the wildflower meadow, sown with the help of the entomologist and botanist Dame Miriam Rothschild, famous for her wildflower gardening at Ashton Wold in Northamptonshire. It was planted with a mix of seed from 32 species in 1982. With the disappearance of working horses, hay meadows had fallen to a mere one per cent of their extent before the Second World War. (The Prince would become an active patron of the wild-flower charity Plantlife after its foundation in 1989.) The wildflower meadow at Highgrove demonstrated what could be done to bring them back. It was also gardened in an interesting way. To establish a wildflower meadow of any kind takes exper-tise, the usual problem being that existing soils are too rich, from previous applications of fertiliser, for thrifty wildflowers that typi-cally thrive where nutrients are thin. At Highgrove, this was made doubly difficult by the Prince's desire to combine colourful corn-cockles, poppies and corn marigolds – the sort of flowers that once grew in cornfields, before farmers could eliminate them using chemicals – with the flora of hay meadows. The conditions needed for each are different: corncockle, for example, having grown up with tillage over the centuries, will only germinate on soil that has been ploughed. According to Rothschild, it was 'his idea entirely' to mix them. The result was not, perhaps, entirely natural but brought Nature in its gayest colours close to the house. As Isabel Bannerman remembers, 'a regime of careful meadow management produced a return of native perennials – wildflowers such as spotted orchids and vetches – and this gradual transformation was very surprising and heartening even to conservationists, long before the "rewilding" experiment on the estate at Knepp Castle in West Sussex in the 2010s and 20s proved something similar.'

This is a book about architecture rather than gardening but, at Highgrove, it is difficult to separate the two. This garden would come to contain many built structures. These give full vent to Charles's love of the Arts and Crafts, and of the fanciful. In a sense they form a garden of ideas, of a kind first developed in the 18th century at Stowe in Buckinghamshire. There the disappointed politician Lord Cobham took out his fury at Sir Robert Walpole's administration by erecting allegorical temples and statues, roundly damning his enemies and promoting his own view of the British constitution. Even if Charles had wanted his garden to become a commentary on current affairs, protocol would have forbidden him such a course. But that was probably far from his mind (the nearest approach to controversy being a statue of Diana, goddess of hunting, in tribute to a favourite recreation as well as his first wife). His instinct was to create something more personal, which would give delight. There are memories of friends, recalled either by name – as in the Shand Gate, incorporating 18th-century Indian doors from Jodhpur, which remembers the Queen's late brother Mark Shand – or in statuary. A bust of Léon Krier, who planned Poundbury, surveys the Cottage Garden from on top of a roughly tooled stone plinth. Busts of Charles's friends and heroes look down from aloft a dry-stone wall – the Duchess of Devonshire, the composer John Tavener, Miriam Rothschild, Kathleen Raine, the Indian environmental activist Vandana Shiva and the former Bishop of London, Richard Chartres. A sculpture of Charles's much-loved Jack Russell Tigga, carved by Marcus Cornish, is set into a lower point of the wall: Tigga had been given to him as a puppy by Lady Salisbury.

There are some Classical sculptures too – such as the bronze *Borghese Gladiator*, given to the Prince by the Marquess of Cholmondeley – which evoke Capability Brown and the Georgian aristocracy's love of the Antique. The true spirit of Highgrove, though, is cosier, more Reptonian, grand in extent but made up of secluded spaces, suffused with Charles's personal brand of charm and wit. There is an intimation of this before the visitor has even entered the estate, in the Cotswold vernacular police box at the gate, dry-stone-walled and with an ogee roof suggesting a policeman's helmet.

Based in Bath, William Bertram had been one of the first architects to receive, disbelievingly, a telephone call from the Prince. He arrived one Saturday morning, to be greeted by Charles, with Tigga at his heels, and shown the garden.

> We walked side by side while he expanded upon his vision for the garden as a whole. I was expecting tentative ideas but it rapidly became clear that all the main structural elements and a good deal of the detail were firmly established in his mind: enclosing yew hedges to form the south garden; pleached limes and more yews to enclose the vista toward the dovecot on the western boundary. Pools, topiary, gates, outbuildings and pavilions. They were all just waiting to be brought forward as sparks which would inspire those with whom he chose to share the design of the garden.

Bertram had been suggested to the Prince by Charles's friend Luke Rittner, then Secretary General of the Arts Council. Charles wanted two little huts to contain beehives on either side of the drawing room terrace; Bertram supplied a Gothic design, with a quatrefoil window, built out of local stone with a slight curve to the roof. There followed a dozen gates and, in 1988, the commission to build a tree house for the young princes. A large holly was selected as the location. True to his Community Architecture beliefs, Charles consulted the end users about their needs before work began; Prince William wanted it 'to be as high as possible so I can get away from everyone,' and reached by a rope ladder. In the end, the rope ladder was supplemented with a conventional one. The idea that the folly might be called Hollyrood House gave Bertram the theme: the balustrade and door and window frames are in the shape of holly leaves.

An important introduction was made by Candida Lycett Green when she took the Prince to see The Ivy, outside Chippenham, 'a capricious architectural starlet of a house,' as Isabel Bannerman described it, built in 1727.[1] Fresh from the History and History of Art course at Edinburgh University, Isabel had restored The Ivy with her husband Julian, whom she had met in Edinburgh where he was working in contemporary art and theatre, and hence the Festival, as well as running a bar on the ground floor of a building he had rescued in the old town. Julian had grown up, the son of gardening parents, in Somerset where he had developed a deep knowledge of antiques and building restoration, 'a haven for those in the 1960s and 1970s who did not fit into other conventional paths through life and who were prepared to graft and use their guile'.[2] He went to the Ruskin School of Art at Oxford but without a grant; to support himself he worked nights at the Randolph Hotel but the strain was too much and eventually he dropped out. The Ivy was a Grade I-listed atoll of architectural bravura amid a sea of housing estates and busy roads. Much praised by the head of English Heritage, Jocelyn Stevens, for its having been rescued without any grant aid, it was interesting enough for the Prince to visit and take tea. He loved all the old baths and radiators and begged the Bannermans to take him to a reclamation yard. The idea of reclamation and re-using old things naturally appealed to the Prince and he asked them to develop a corner of the Highgrove garden for what academics call 'spolia'. Limestone blocks and inscriptions were scattered among ferns in the manner of the poet and gardener Ian Hamilton Finlay, with whom Julian had worked in his Edinburgh years. The next request was somehow to enhance the junction of the formal rose garden and meadow. Searching the reclamation yards again, they found a pair of handsome 1900 factory gates in iron and remodelled them into a single garden gate with fixed side panels, adding repoussé leaves and the Prince of Wales's feathers to give them a bit of royal elan.

The fernery led to a commission to build a green oak temple, inspired by a tourist souvenir of the Doric temple at Agrigento which the Bannermans had bought when visiting Sicily in 1995. Taking the form of a cork model, like a cruder version of the models in the Soane Museum, it simplified the forms of the architecture, making them rounder and more rustic.

> Pretty basic though it is, this model is somehow imbued with a genius quality … We realised that by rendering part of [our] temple with coloured lime wash, it would be something like building a half-timbered classical temple, or the Tudor-style Pitchford Tree House.

Once the oak blocks of which it consisted had been assembled, they were distressed by the application of a chainsaw and wire brush. The tympanum was filled with pieces of extravagantly weathered wood in the shape of ancient Caledonian pine from lochs flooded for hydro-electric schemes that Julian Bannerman knew in Scotland and collected by lorry.

The Bannermans' principal contribution to Highgrove is the

Fountain made from old pieces of stone from Hereford Cathedral and planted with gunnera as the centrepiece of the stumpery, created by Isabel and Julian Bannerman in 1996. Containing the stumps of 180 sweet chestnut trees, the stumpery takes its inspiration from the 18th century.

stumpery. This celebrates the Romantic taste for what Horace Walpole called 'gloomth', coined to describe the Gothick ambiance of Strawberry Hill. While some Georgians enjoyed the morbid frisson experienced in damp and dripping grottoes, architects such as William Kent, in Merlin's Cave, or Thomas Wright, designer of the Hermitage at Badminton, created similarly dark effects by means that, says Isabel Bannerman, were 'warm and dry'. They used gnarled wood from 'really beautiful veteran sweet chestnut, elms and oaks'. These were followed in the Victorian period by the great stumpery at Biddulph Grange in Staffordshire, where the owner John Bateman created a garden reflecting his belief in the Biblical story of Creation.

The stumpery at Highgrove was made from the stumps of 180

largely sweet chestnuts, from Cowdray Park where trees of great age had been felled to make ammunition boxes during the Second World War. 'Chestnut stumps rot down to leave a starfish-shape of very hard wood, having been compressed by the weight of the whole enormous tree upon the base such as is used for the stocks of shot guns.' In due course the stumpery became home to Highgrove's National Collection of hostas.

Originally the idea had been to create a *campo santo* with three temples; the budget, however, only ran to two, with inscriptions, surrounded by rustic fortifications made from sweet chestnut roots. Later the stumpery was extended to include a rustic pyramid of vermiculated green oak, originally a homage to Ted Hughes and bearing a plaque by his friend, the American sculptor and graphic artist Leonard Baskin. Showing Hughes in profile with a crow and a pike, this was given to Charles on Hughes's death by the poet's widow. When his beloved grandmother the Queen Mother died five years later, the Prince worked with the Bannermans during the two-week mourning period, adding a pool with a fountain made from stone from Hereford Cathedral, the water of which emerges through a planting of gunnera. The plaque to Hughes has since been moved and replaced with a relief of the Queen Mother, displayed in front of a starburst referencing the Burma or Garter Star, although the effect recalls the halo usually associated with Christian saints. Some have questioned the artistic quality of the piece, even to the extent of calling it kitsch – but that is not the point: the setting is not a sculpture gallery but a garden of memory. 'When Camilla got engaged to *Principe*, I gave my best snowdrops – really tall ones – and put them all around,' remembers Julian. 'They're still there.'

Another Bannerman inspiration took the form of a gilded phoenix, made from welded steel strips. It was placed on top of a column from Waterloo station which Charles had been given

Charles built the Sanctuary at Highgrove as a place of calm contemplation and will spend time there whenever he returns home. It is built from the traditional materials that the King loves and includes proto-Classical elements.

and erected at the end of an avenue of lime trees. The Bannermans' original idea had been a stork, resting on a nest of twigs and royal oak leaves. However, this naturally morphed into a phoenix rising from the ashes, given that its appearance coincided with the foundation of the Phoenix Trust for architectural restoration.

In 2008 the majestic cedar of Lebanon, for which Charles had developed 'an instant passion' on first seeing the house, was found unsafe due to honey fungus and had to be felled. Devastated by the loss, Charles wanted to honour the tree and mark its passing. This time, he chose Mark Hoare, whom he knew from his work on the Sanctuary, to design a monument. As Hoare remembers, 'HRH's deep connection to the tree and the idea of marking it in a slightly reverential way is at the heart of it. It was a gravestone for a tree, but at the same time really quirky and fun.' A spire – in dialogue with the spire of Tetbury church, a few miles away – rises to the height of the old cedar. Since wood from a cedar of Lebanon is only suitable for use inside a building, it is built out of oak and rises above an undulating roof of oak which covers the remains of the cedar's trunk; the Prince used a surviving limb of the tree to hang bird feeders on, until it became overgrown. A gap was left in the roof so that an oak sapling which had taken root next to the cedar could grow through it – once it was big enough, the spire could be removed. That, at least, was the original thought: the spire has itself become such a feature of the garden that it is unlikely to happen. The oak and the spire will probably co-exist until the pavilion falls apart.

Delightful as a caprice, the Oak Pavilion is also a demonstration of Harmony. The same comment could be made of the whole garden, which might indeed be seen as the fullest expression of the Prince's philosophy. This was not always the case. In the early years, there seemed to be too many ideas. They were as restless as the Prince himself appeared to be in the later stages of his first marriage. Like Poundbury in its early phase, the garden suffered from the Prince's enthusiasm for the many gardeners and craftsmen he met; it seemed as though each had to be given a project, regardless of whether it would sit happily with what already existed. There was a rapid churn of advisors. A less complicated project might have exuded a greater degree of peacefulness. In 2009, returning for the first time for nine years, Sir Roy Strong found that it remained 'fragmentary and unresolved ... confused and lacking cohesion, going off at tangents all over the place'.[3] But in this respect Highgrove has changed. The garden has been overtaken by the first principle of Harmony – reverence for Nature – and, as a result, has become truly original. The density of the vegetation means that you cannot take in all the different elements at a glance. On Charles's orders, nothing can be cut down unless out of direst necessity. Trees grow and decay to the slow cycle of Nature. Age takes its toll, they become smothered in creepers. The stumps of the stumpery are eloquent of life's natural journey, as they rot away.

Of course, as in any garden, the planting scheme changes. An enthusiasm for delphiniums one year will be replaced by another horticultural must-have the next. These are things to delight the eye of a painter. 'The flowers in the garden are a reflection of the stars in the sky,' read the Egyptian hieroglyphics over a doorway in the garden, carved by students from the Prince's Foundation (translation courtesy of the Highgrove guidebook); and the Highgrove flowers are as beautiful as they are numerous. But there are also places where the experience is akin to stumbling through a jungle and accidentally falling upon the remains of a lost civilisation. The vegetation has been allowed to take over. Intervention has been kept to a minimum. As the many copper beech trees – Highgrove holds the national collection – grow to maturity, the garden will risk becoming a wood. Already the house itself all but disappears in autumn beneath a number of creepers with giant leaves. The result is amazing, wonderful and slightly scary, as though Highgrove House has become Hansel and Gretel's cottage in the woods. There is a memory here of Ashton Wold, Miriam Rothschild's country house in Northamptonshire which was similarly engulfed. When asked by Julian Bannerman why he did not do something about the magnolia next to Highgrove, the Prince replied: 'It's really good because you can hide inside the house and nobody can see you but you can look out.' Highgrove may not be original in all respects and it incorporates the ideas of many people, but some aspects of the vision are highly personal, only to be compared, perhaps, to the garden of ruins that the Surrealist patron Edward James made for himself in the Mexican jungle.

The Oak Pavilion commemorates a majestic cedar of Lebanon that had to be felled in 2008. The oak spire reaches the height of the original tree, creating, in the words of the architect Mark Hoare, 'a gravestone that is at the same time really quirky and fun.'

Like any garden, Highgrove is a human creation, and the effects we see are only there because they have been allowed to develop; nearly a dozen gardeners hold the balance between decay and dissolution, not to mention keeping invasive weeds at bay in an organic garden from which chemical weedkillers have been banished. But for all that, the effect – to the eye of a conventional gardener – could seem pretty weird, hardly gardening at all. Which is part of the point. This garden is not simply about extracting beauty from the myriad of plants available from modern suppliers. To quote the Prince, it 'really does spring from my heart and, strange as it may seem to some, creating it has been rather like a form of worship'. Harmony rules.

SEVEN

UTOPIA

Poundbury

S TAFF IN THE DUCHY OF CORNWALL OFFICES AT
10 Buckingham Gate used not to refer to Charles by
his usual title. To them he was Twenty-four. 'Prince of
Wales' would have been too much of a mouthful while the shorthand 'HRH' would have caused confusion, given the number of
HRHs who passed in and out. But only he was the 24th Duke
of Cornwall. Once his successor, William, the present Prince of
Wales, was on the scene, it was clear there would one day be a
Twenty-five. These numbers demonstrate the great age of an
institution established in 1337 as an estate to fund the monarch's
eldest son until he became king; the first recipient of its income
was Edward III's son, the Black Prince. The Duchy had owned
land in Dorset since the 14th century. The ridge to the west of
Dorchester, the county town, where Poundbury and Middle
Farms were located, had always been farmed, but the building of
a bypass in the late 1980s made it a natural development site. It
was Dorset County Council who approached the Duchy about
building homes on it.

If only the Duchy of Cornwall would build something modern,

Michael Manser, President of the RIBA, had said after the Hampton Court speech – implying that it was all very well for Charles to carp from the sidelines of architecture but that he would not find it so easy if he got stuck in himself. Within a short time the Prince had picked up the gauntlet. The Duchy, under his chairmanship, would create not just one building but a major new settlement on 400 acres of land outside Dorchester. Called Poundbury, it would not be modern in Manser's stylistic sense: no tower blocks, no elevated walks, no concrete and plate glass. It would, however, be modern – radically so – in addressing the big issues in contemporary planning, which most developers and architects had ignored. The project was announced in 1988, the year after the Mansion House speech. By 2024 it has become a settlement of 4,600 people in over 2,300 homes. After more than 30 years, building is projected to finish by 2028.

A Prince who is known for bashing architects cannot be surprised when the profession unites to belittle his efforts as a patron of building. In this case, critical architects were joined by media pundits and the *bien pensants* of London dinner parties. Often, the denigrators had not seen what they were talking about. Those who did go, in the early days, needed to visualise what had yet to be built, rather than judge the initial scattering of over-designed little buildings which could be described, with some justification, as an architectural theme park. To their credit, the Prince and the Duchy refused to be blown off course. Now that Poundbury is finished, it can be appreciated as that rare thing: a large new settlement completed to the masterplan – and under the same masterplanner – that had been in place 30 years before. There were battles along the way, battles hard fought – with officialdom; with journalists; with pontificating architects; with, in the early days, the Council of the Duchy of Cornwall itself. But all the original objectives have been fulfilled, and the best possible judgement on Poundbury is the one passed by the people who live there. They love it.

The masterplanner was Léon Krier. Krier is now famous around the world for his work on new settlements and as an architectural theorist. In the 1980s, however, he was by no means an obvious choice for the Prince, let alone the conservative Duchy council. Born in Luxembourg, multilingual and a brilliant pianist, Krier is the very image of a type that does not exist much in Britain – the intellectual. He is a master of metaphor and unrivalled for his ability to condense his arguments into cartoon-like drawings

Léon Krier, wearing trademark scarf, with the Prince and the architect John Thompson, whom the Prince had known since Cambridge. The occasion was the first public consultation on the proposed development of Poundbury Farm which took place on a sunny June day in 1989.

which ridicule opposing views; he charms those who agree with him, but he does not compromise with those who do not. To the upper echelons of the Duchy, to whom Charles now introduced him, he was an unknown quantity, somewhat alarming in his radicalism and beyond their previous ken. Even his clothes, chosen for his home in the South of France rather than rural Dorset, with a silk scarf thrown over his shoulder even on England's hottest of days, signalled a Continental point of view. No country tweeds for Krier. He was not only an intellectual but metropolitan, which was possibly worse.

'I am an architect,' Krier famously said, 'because I don't build.' Technically he was not an architect, having never finished his studies. After a year at the University of Stuttgart, he had left to join the London office of James Stirling – the darling of the British Modernist establishment, famous for beautifully conceived buildings that were disastrous for those using them (the cascading glass wall of the History Faculty building in Cambridge was plagued by leaks in wet weather and fried those behind it in summer). Stirling had run foul of the Prince for demolishing the Mappin & Webb building along with other ornate Victorian shops along Poultry, which he replaced with one of his less brilliant works, a lumpish design which overpowers the corner on which it stands. During the four years that he worked for Big Jim, as Stirling was known, Krier developed a growing hatred for the pretentiousness and conceit of Modern architecture. On leaving, he condemned himself to a 20-year period in the doldrums, teaching at the progressive, anarchic Architectural Association and at the Royal College of Art, while forever decrying the principles of Modernism. Hence his comment about not building: architects who did get their work built were not worthy of the name. He cast himself instead as a prophet crying in the wilderness, and had it not been for the Prince of Wales's Hampton

Court speech he might have remained there. Now, though, his Messiah had come.

On reading about Hampton Court, Krier sent Charles details of a project for Washington DC which would have turned the American capital into 'a kind of Classical marvel'. It was noted; the Prince returned thanks. But nothing more happened until the *Real Architecture* exhibition opened at the Building Centre in 1987. In it, Krier showed a scheme for the redevelopment of Spitalfields Market which had been well received by the press. As we know, the Prince opened the exhibition – and he already knew everything he needed to know about Spitalfields. As Krier remembers, he said:

> 'Let's talk.' So we talked and he said 'would you like to be my consultant on architecture, particularly on urbanism?', and I said, 'Wow, my God!' How could I refuse? And then we'd meet for six to seven months, always at strange times and places, like at 3 o'clock in the morning with some Russian princess in Chelsea or some cottage somewhere on his properties. It had to be hush-hush. I became the consultant for Paternoster Square.

In March 1988 he wrote an article for Roger Scruton's magazine *Modern Painters* entitled 'God Save the Prince', republished as 'God Save the King' in Charles Jencks's *The Prince and the Architects*.

> The thought that Queen Elizabeth II will be chiefly remembered by the worst kind of architecture and urbanism which the country has produced in its history is duly alarming the future King. In the Mansion House address his voice had an almost desperate, even tragic ring. If he were the romantic dreamer which critics make him out to be, wouldn't he be

better off enjoying day-dreams and wealth in comfortable retirement? Instead, like no one else in the public arena, he reminds us of the possibilities and duties of architecture not as the expression of present market forces but as the prime instrument for realising cities and landscapes where life is worth living.

Later that year, Krier was in the United States, where he was working with Duany Plater-Zyberk on Seaside, Florida. While he was there, a call came from the Prince of Wales appointing him as the masterplanner for Poundbury.

Krier's masterplan seemed to be as foreign as he was himself. On the Continent, people often prefer to live in towns and cities, a legacy, perhaps, of the city walls that remained standing long after they had been demolished in Britain; constrained by the walls, the urban spaces were crammed with people, living in close proximity to each other, and consequently buzzed with life. After the Second World War, the countryside lost population. In common with other Northern Europeans, the British, or so it used to be said, hanker after a private if not solitary existence in the countryside; if they cannot get it, they wall themselves up behind the privet hedges of invincible green suburbs (attitudes have changed now that Britain's cities are more cosmopolitan, easier to get around and less polluted. There are also coffee shops). Krier proposed that Poundbury would not be a suburb but an urban extension of the town, somewhere that would be, for most purposes, a self-sufficient entity, rather than having to rely for everyday existence on the services in Dorchester. This was a revolutionary idea in terms of late 20th-century planning.

For one thing, it meant providing infrastructure before most of the development had even begun – an upfront cost for the Duchy. Krier's drawing showed public buildings, town squares and tree-lined avenues from which there would be no obvious financial return. This alone might have killed the scheme, given that the Prince of Wales chairs a Duchy Council made up of people who are experienced in land management and investing, and charged by Parliament with making an adequate return on the portfolio. The Prince cannot order them what to do – in a typically British way, he must work through influence. However, he and Krier were able to persuade them that the long-term return from the new approach would ultimately make more money for the Duchy than a conventional development. By playing the long game, they could take advantage of a rising market. More money had to be committed at the beginning of the project but land values would increase during the course of construction, more than compensating for the initial expenditure. Thirty years on, this has proved to be the case. It was not obvious, however, in the late 1980s.

Poundbury would be somewhere that inhabitants both lived and worked. This was another challenge to the planning orthodoxy of the day. Since the Industrial Revolution, work for many ordinary folk had meant grime, noise and smoking chimneys; nobody wanted to live next door to a factory. During the Thatcher decade it became clear that Britain's future did not lie with manufacturing, but the notion that work and domestic life should occupy different zones had become ingrained. There was more to come. Roads came before houses and traffic engineers ruled the roost; the safest way to manage cars and lorries was to give their drivers maximum visibility and a clear run. Main roads should therefore curve gently: nothing should be placed beside them that might obstruct the line of sight. Once these roads had been established, the majority of houses would be disposed around lollypop-like cul-de-sacs, with turning circles at the bottom – again for the benefit of motorists. Garage doors would be a prominent architectural feature. Poundbury turned these assumptions on their head. The object was to create human interaction rather than free vehicle movement. Cars were not banished – who in the countryside does not need one? – but kept off the streets and out of sight. Parking was consigned to courts behind the houses. Rather than facilitating the movement of cars through the streets, streets were planned in such a way as to slow them down.

The person responsible for the road layout at Poundbury was Andrew Cameron, a young engineer, with a background in architecture as well as highways, then working for the structural engineer Alan Baxter. As he remembers:

> The places people like to visit on holiday are often to be enjoyed on foot. The streets might be narrow and twisty. We took the view that streets of different widths, where drivers were less certain how to proceed, would slow traffic by themselves, without the need for signs. They could find their way cautiously through the centre of the development rather than just whizz around the outside. Nobody was doing this at the time. Everyone else was following the standard guidance as set out in the Department of Transport's Design Bulletin 32, issued in 1977.

Poundbury overturned the conventional wisdom on this key aspect of planning. Road markings and signage are kept to a minimum, so that drivers have to think as they make their way along. The octagonal Buttercross partially occupies the roadway of the Bridport Road: cars have to slow down to get around it. Incredibly, before Poundbury it had become impossible for architects to create that most popular element of the English town – a square. Road junctions required roundabouts or, at the very least, traffic lights; DB32 deemed that crossroads were otherwise too dangerous.

Poundbury has squares – lots of them. 'The kerb follows the architecture rather than the roadway, leaving the centre for people to meet each other and children to play. This was revolutionary.'

There was another way in which the method of development at Poundbury would be entirely different from the prevailing norm. Ever since the Garden City Movement had taken British planning by storm at the beginning of the 20th century, it had been assumed that more space per person equalled greater human contentment. But where the population of a development is too scattered, it lacks the critical mass to support shops, cafes, pubs and other local services; they are then located so far away that the only way of reaching them is by car – thus perpetuating an evil. Krier believed that for most people it is more important to be surrounded by all the liveliness of a traditional town than to have an extra few square feet of garden. To increase the density, he proposed reintroducing one of the most familiar building types in the English village: the terrace. Terraced houses are cheaper to build than free-standing ones, as well as being more energy-efficient. In traditional towns and villages throughout Britain, they stand directly on the street; but modern planners expected them to stand back from the street behind scraps of front garden – what on earth for? Another thing: there would be a range of different types of accommodation, so that residents who came to Poundbury as young parents, taking advantage of the local schools, could stay in Poundbury until they entered sheltered housing in old age. And a third of the new housing would be affordable housing – only nobody would know where it was; externally it would look exactly the same as the homes sold at market prices, so there would be no stigma attached.

Above all, everything people might need would be within a short stroll. They could walk to shops, walk to work, walk to places to have a drink, to socialise, to enjoy the fresh air. Children could walk to school and play outside. Some facilities would be further away than others but nowhere beyond a 15-minute walk. Walking is good for health, good for well-being and it builds community. Because when people are outside the house and outside their vehicles, they are more likely to run into neighbours and enjoy those friendly interactions which are part of the joy of local life, when it is properly run.

Notice that nothing yet has been said about architectural style. Although virtually all the criticism of Poundbury has centred on its 'toy town' appearance, the look of the place is far from the whole story. Poundbury happens to be in a vernacular and Classical idiom (the Classical ornament being reserved for the more prestigious buildings, according to the principle of hierarchy that was one of the 'Ten Commandments' of *A Vision of Britain*). As we have seen, Charles is no fan of Modernism, which is naturally suited to large monoliths rather than streets of small houses and blocks; whatever had been the case in the 1950s and 1960s, by the 1980s housing was not attracting the best Modernist talent. But Poundbury could have been built in a different style from the one chosen without the fundamental principles being affected. Unfortunately it was not those principles that received the bulk of media attention.

After a year, Krier's design was ready. It was remarkable for the succession of piazzas and public buildings, linked by tree-lined streets, somewhat as though it was a modern-day Pienza sprung from the mind of a Renaissance pope.

In one way the Duchy was lucky with Poundbury's location. As well as sitting beneath the gaze of the Iron Age fort of Maiden Castle, it comes under the aegis of West Dorset District Council. West Dorset may not have had recent experience of Renaissance utopianism but was blessed with a visionary district architect in David Oliver, who believed that there must be a more sympathetic alternative to the standard housing types provided by the volume house builders. His instinct had already been proved right in two village extensions. At Abbotsbury and Broadwindsor, local house builders had been able to create homes in the spirit of the National Trust's cottage at Higher Brockhampton, a vernacular cottage in a typically West Dorset mix of materials, including thatch, which happens to be where the great West Country writer Thomas Hardy was born. The Duchy poached Oliver to advise on Poundbury's local aesthetic. It had also been trialling the Prince of Wales's ideas in several small proto-Poundbury projects, such as Thicket Mead, in the former mining town of Midsomer Norton in Somerset; proposed as a Baroque scheme it morphed into a more irregular design to increase housing density. Field Farm, which added 600 new houses to Shepton Mallet, where the Duchy worked with a local landowner, was another precursor to Poundbury. Masterplanning was then a new discipline, with little precedent to follow. 'We had to work it out for ourselves,' says Robert Adam of ADAM Architecture, the lead architect of Midsomer Norton and Shepton Mallet. 'Observation was important – a close study of the local vernacular. Otherwise it was a matter of thinking it through.'

Despite these toe-in-the-water initiatives, the Duchy remained suspicious of Krier, whose vision, however beguiling, was untried and looked expensive. The Council appointed the surveyors Drivers Jonas to oversee the project and rein Krier in. That was not Krier's idea. He met Christopher Jonas at Highgrove and joined the Prince around the big dining table to look at plans. According to Krier,

Jonas said: 'Yes, Sir, we will of course take on board what Mr Krier says.' Whereupon the Prince banged his fist on the table and replied: 'Christopher, you are not going to take on board

Sheep continue to graze the Great Field at Poundbury, as they did when it was farm-land. Behind can be seen homes of different sizes, in vernacular styles: there is no visual difference between affordable accommodation and that sold at market rates.

what Leo says, you are going to do what he tells you.' From then on it was open war. He called me from everywhere saying, 'You can't do this.' And I'd say, 'You have to do it. The Prince wants it and he is The Boss.'

Behind the scenes, the temperature would remain high for some time. Figures were presented to show that the Krier scheme would cost tens of millions more than the Duchy could justify; Krier would take them away and have them reanalysed – returning to argue that the costs would be much lower than had been presented, because some of the public architecture would be off budget, being paid for by sponsors. (This did not happen. Only one sponsor – Andrew Brownsword – could be reeled in.) An alternative scheme was drawn up using William Bertram as architect, but Charles rejected it.

By June 1989, it was time to ask the public what they thought. The sun shone and the consultation took place in a marquee beneath the tall trees of Poundbury Farm. Krier wore a light-coloured suit with the trademark silk scarf knotted around his neck; an enthusiastic young Liam O'Connor, who would go on to be architect of many Classical monuments in Britain and Normandy, served as his assistant. The event was run by the Community Architect John Thompson, whom Charles had known at Cambridge. The tent was packed. Remembered by his friend, the poet Ian McMillan, as 'charismatic and ever-enthusiastic under a cloud of curly hair,' Thompson would be one of the founding trustees of the Prince of Wales's Institute of Architecture. However, he found it no easier to manage Krier than the Duchy had. 'Léon is going to talk to you briefly about what he has prepared and then we get on to serious business,' Krier remembers him as announcing.

So he gave me ten minutes to talk. So when I started, and I already knew a lot of people there, I said: 'Well John wants to give me ten minutes but I need an hour because this is over a year's work and ten minutes won't do it.' So I asked for a vote, 'Do I talk now or does he win?' And they all stood up and went 'Yeah!'

There was another meeting in the Dorchester Corn Exchange. It was felt, reasonably, that Krier's first design did not owe enough to the local vernacular tradition and Krier revised it, with the help of Oliver, promising that local architects would be employed to bring their knowledge of Dorset to bear.

This did nothing to reassure the architectural establishment in London, led by the President of the RIBA Max Hutchinson. Local people, on the other hand, 'once they had recovered from

Woodlands Crescent, begun in 2003 and finished 2006, was designed in a restrained late-Georgian style by Ben Pentreath. The repetition of simple elements creates a sense of calm, setting the tone for the later phases of Poundbury. Details such as the iron railings, granite kerbstones and abundant planting would not be found in most housing estates.

the initial shock of encountering something so different from the normal pattern of development,' were mostly won round. The consultation process continued. Sometimes the Prince of Wales, arriving by helicopter, would drop in on the meetings unannounced. Planning consent for the first 7.5 hectares (Phase 1) was obtained in 1991 but it was a disastrous time for the property market, when the golden years of the Lawson Boom ended in an equally spectacular Bust. The engineer and urban designer Alan Baxter was appointed to work with Krier to keep the architectural vision within the bounds of economic reality. He was a good choice; they did not fall out. Designs were swapped by fax machine. Together they decided on details such as the placing of lamp posts, or – better – where lamps should be attached to walls, avoiding the need for a post; usually such matters were the preserve of lighting engineers who were trained in lumens rather than visual appearance. Another practical move was to secure Andrew Hamilton as development director: he had previously worked for Haslemere Estates, the developers of Richmond Riverside, so had practical experience of running large building projects while being onside with the ideology (paradoxically, 'traditional' in terms of architecture had become 'alternative' in terms of the business world). Hamilton has overseen the realisation of Charles's dream ever since. Even so, Poundbury would have to wait until 1993 before ground was broken.

Over the next three years, Phase 1 delivered nearly 200 houses and over 50 flats, including 55 social housing units rented through the Guinness Trust, built by the local companies CG Fry & Son of Litton Cheney and Morrish Builders of Poole. The Guinness Trust units, offered to people on the local authority's social housing list at £55–60 per week, provided a way forward during a deep recession when most market house builders had drawn in their horns. In Poundbury jargon, they were pepper-potted (that is, dotted) among the other types of housing, which were for sale. As Hamilton later recalled, 'House builders said "We can't build private houses next to social houses, they won't sell." We have proved that this is not true.'

Ben Pentreath, who, years later, would be one of the principal architects at Poundbury, visited with a group from the Institute at a time when only the first few buildings had gone up. It was a 'surreal experience' to leave Dorchester, still recognisably the town that Thomas Hardy had immortalised as Casterbridge, and cross the hinterland of suburban streets that had been built in the 1950s. There they found 'a little white terrace of social flats', designed by Peterjohn Smyth from Esha Architects. Smyth was the coordinating architect for Phase 1 of Poundbury. Built of vernacular brick, his Dorchester Hospital, with its red and blue doors and windows, had been given the Prince's seal of approval in *A Vision of Britain*. Next to the terrace 'the first little Georgian-style stone-built cottages stood all alone in the middle of a muddy field that had recently been farmland and was now a weird building site'. Pentreath and his friends had student projects to get on with, in Pentreath's case designing a pub. Other students would come in 2000 to construct a Millennium Belvedere. But since the Institute was regarded as 'zany, academic and not quite practical enough,' contact between it and the Duchy was limited.

The heart of this first small phase of the development was Pummery Square, an extraordinary space in comparison to the provision of most volume house-building schemes, perhaps too lavish for the Poundbury that was then under construction, although it now makes perfect sense. John Simpson designed a market building – Brownsword Hall – to act as a village hall, funded by the greetings card entrepreneur Andrew Brownsword. Stubby stone columns are combined with a dramatically deep roof with tall pointed gables which has a Germanic, even Expressionist air. Behind the hall, water trickles into a stone field trough from a ram's head, the whole composition framed by an elegant stone arch – rustic but with a flavour of Rome.

Throughout the countryside, pubs were closing at an alarming rate: the drink-driving laws made it difficult for publicans in remote places to maintain their old trade. But here at Poundbury a new pub opened; it is called the Poet Laureate after Ted Hughes, the elementally craggy Yorkshire poet whose bust stands in the Highgrove garden – Charles and Hughes would go on long night walks together across Dartmoor, talking philosophy. The pub sign originally bore his portrait. A Spar Convenience Store is discreetly located behind a colonnade and labelled 'Poundbury Village Stores'. Both pub and supermarket were designed by Pentreath, saving the Duchy money while also giving a talented youngster a break.

Opposite the Poet Laureate's side elevation stands the Octagon Cafe, in, as its name suggests, an octagonal pavilion with traditional French windows and fanlights: charm personified. In 1994, to the joy of those close to the project, the Stitchinghouse Design shop opened: the first cottage industry whose owner, Sue McCarthy-Moore, both lived and worked in Poundbury. This was how Poundbury was meant to be.

In relation to Poundbury as a whole, Phase 1 was tiny. But naturally the Prince's involvement caused it to attract a disproportionate degree of press comment. Sympathetic journalists felt that it got close to vindicating the Prince's views. Here they could see beguiling streets, architecturally varied and built of attractive materials, with a certain amount of ornament and some lovely eyecatchers like the Octagon. It was not a royal plaything but a soundly costed commercial proposition, which satisfied the stringent financial expectations of the Duchy Council. Rather than emulating the Classical marvel that Krier had wanted to create in Washington DC, the ambition was modest: to build streets of varied architecture that people would enjoy living in. But to do even this was, surely, a species of English miracle. Nothing of this quality and inventiveness had been seen in Britain for 50 years. There was, perhaps, too much going on, a criticism that might have been made of the Highgrove garden as it then was. While Dorchester is a relatively low-key county town, Poundbury Phase 1 was crowded with architects (mostly local at this stage) and London consultants working next door to each other, creating a knickerbocker glory of different styles. Stomachs used to the seed cake of most traditional townscapes found it too rich to digest. This can be blamed on the Prince's enthusiasm. He energetically sought out architects who reflected his ideas, met them on his travels around Britain and kept their names on a list. Although short in relation to the total number of architects in the country, it was long enough to provide a quarry of talent, ready to be commissioned when the next project came up. It was a forgivable fault. Niche architects were encouraged, their work given exposure, the development saved from the curse of sameyness. But it led to the feeling that this was an architectural capriccio; ordinary people might not seem to fit in.

Or so one feared at the time. Time has since then worked its magic. Overly colourful walls had become duller, mottled with green. The gloss of newness has rubbed off. Maintenance is required here and there, as it always will be where the window frames are made of wood (not just an aesthetic preference: they are now seen as greener than PVC and the demand from Poundbury has driven manufacturers to increase the specification in terms of draft-proofing. All the windows at Poundbury are double-glazed.) Poundbury has settled down. Walking around, visitors may feel as they do when visiting historic towns. Whatever the Classical elements (generally not very pronounced) it is really in the great English tradition of the Picturesque, the movement that gave rise to the landscape park in the 18th century and has influenced aspects of British planning (through the idea that ill-assorted elements will rub along) ever since. Today, Poundbury unfolds in a series of views, each of which can make watercolourists long to reach for the paints. An architectural historian might know that some of the buildings can only have been designed at the turn of the 21st century but it may be far from obvious to other people. Harmony is back on her throne.

By the time the Queen and Duke of Edinburgh paid their first visit to Poundbury in 1998, it had an established identity. Dorchester taxi drivers were calling it Charlieville. The royal couple may have been as struck by what they did not see as what they did. No visible television aerials, satellite dishes or telephone wires. No frosted glass, even for residents exasperated by the number of visitors who peered through their windows. No people of his own age, according to a 20-year-old car mechanic, living with his parents, whose family found it difficult to park their three cars. Poundbury did not yet fulfil the Prince's ideal of a fully integrated community of different generations; as time went on and prices rose, it would appeal strongly to old buyers with more spending power than first-timers. (This changed when a local primary school opened and a secondary school moved to the edge of Poundbury from Dorchester; now the playgrounds are well patronised.) There was no time for the Queen and her husband to visit the computer firm established in a group of old barns that had survived from the original farm or the factory for Dorchester Chocolates, now owned by Charbonnel et Walker. Dorset Cereals, later bought by Associated British Foods, would become another food brand successfully established in Poundbury.

But as yet the development was on the scale of a model village, not an ideal town. It seemed that Phase 2, begun in 1999, might not require such a high level of input. There was no longer the need for kerbstones and street furniture to be positioned by expensive consultants from London. The idiom had been set and it was assumed that later phases could be rolled out with less supervision of the visual content. The Duchy commissioned designs for houses from the large number of architects who had caught the Prince's eye. Developers then tendered to build them, in conformity with the drawings. For a time, the direction seemed to wobble. Details lost their edge. While about 900 dwellings and six hectares of employment space were provided over the next decade, Charles was not entirely happy with the result. It was time for a reset. This was provided by the decision to employ a much smaller team of architects – largely Ben Pentreath and George Saumarez Smith, with additional contributions from Craig Hamilton - in the South-West Quadrant, developed from 2006. Together they designed the remaining townscape in a varied but unfussy Georgian style. To quote Pentreath,

> People can cope with a lot of very simple repetition. No-one is walking around the Georgian part of Islington getting bored. No-one is walking around Edinburgh wishing for more variety. It's a single typology, a single material, a single building identity. Yes, you and I as architectural historians can get excited about the difference between a railing detail of 1770 and 1810 or this is Roman and this is Greek. But as a fundamental vision, the New Town of Edinburgh, which would be on a plan about triple the size of Poundbury, is just a single architectural vision. For house builders, repetition is a lot easier to do, and it's also less expensive.

Poundbury Phases 3 and 4 followed the example of the South-West Quadrant. Poundbury was back on track. The long Buttermarket square, with the octagonal Buttercross at the higher

Opened in 2016, Queen Mother Square forms the grand centrepiece of Poundbury. This may leave Dorchester – the architecturally modest county town to which Poundbury is attached – in the shade. But by any standards, it is a striking achievement of contemporary urbanism and as pleasant a place to visit as many of the Continental towns from which it takes inspiration.

northern end and Craig Hamilton's Ionic Maiden House facing it lower down, set a new standard of urban composition.

By the time HM the Queen returned in 2016, the plan had been all but achieved. Pummery Square had been a local centre; the main civic centre was Queen Mother Square, focused on a statue of the Prince's grandmother and surrounded by grand classical buildings. With Charles's support, Classicism had come a long way since the 1980s, when it gave the impression of being a small if not loony cult. Here was an apartment building (Strathmore House) with an arcaded ground floor supporting a giant Corinthian order, with capitals based on St Paul's Cathedral; Francis Terry gave *trompe l'oeil* columns to a side and back façade which would have otherwise been left blank. Here, astonishingly, was the Duchess of Cornwall Inn, which uses the Doric, Ionic and Corinthian orders stacked one on top of the other, as though this were Venice. (The latter was not an easy trick for Quinlan and Francis Terry to pull off. As the elder Terry describes in *The Layman's Guide to Classical Architecture*, 2022, adjusting the elements of the three orders so that they fitted comfortably together required care.) Léon Krier's masterplan called for a tower and, lo, one would soon arise from the pencil of Ben Pentreath. The tower belonged to Royal Pavilion, named after one of the Queen Mother's racehorses. Inside the Pavilion are large and swanky flats, one a penthouse, some with large balconies, reached by a grand communal entrance hall with a concierge. On a Monopoly board, this would be Poundbury's Park Lane. Kings Point House contains a Waitrose supermarket – the only brand-name shop in this place of small family businesses except for the Pummery Square Spar. As Charles contemplated the fruit of more than 20 years of construction, he might have thought of Wotan's words as he awakes from a dream of Valhalla at the opening of Wagner's Ring Cycle, 'The everlasting work is finished.'

With the Queen's visit, attitudes in the media began to change. Even the *Guardian*, no friend to royalty and a persistent critic of Poundbury, published an article by Oliver Wainwright under the heading 'A ROYAL REVOLUTION: IS PRINCE CHARLES'S MODEL VILLAGE HAVING THE LAST LAUGH?' Yes, one could say that it was. Despite the evil predictions of the doom-sayers at the start of the project, it is now, according to the Duchy website,

> home to some 4,600 people in a mix of private and affordable housing, Poundbury also provides employment for over 2,600 people working in more than 250 shops, cafés, offices and factories. A further 200 are employed in construction across the site and many more are self employed and occasionally work from home.

With sports pitches, numerous meeting places, family-owned shops and a community farm, Poundbury offers a barely believable, happily-ever-after lifestyle of a type that fairy stories are made of in the early 21st century. The built environment, whether or not to everyone's taste, was carefully planned, meticulously designed (over-designed in places, some might say) and soundly built; unlike a conventional housing scheme, which the volume house builder will sell off as soon as possible, disclaiming all future responsibility, the Duchy remains involved to curate the detail of the place, ensuring that its special quality is maintained for future residents down the generations. None of this would have been possible without the personal commitment of Twenty-four. Having braved the opposition of the Duchy Council and others and suffered decades of flak from the media, he has visited at least twice every year since the project's inception. These are not merely face-showing, hand-shaking occasions. Everyone who accompanies him testifies to his attention to detail. He will notice things that even the architects have missed. Back at Highgrove, one of his pleasures is to look through the architects' drawings that he is sent to approve. Each one has to be signed off by The Boss himself before it can go into construction. As Krier puts it, 'This man is really unique.'

None of this is to say that Poundbury is without fault. Architecturally it was at times over-egged. It would benefit from a church spire to give it focus. The weirdness that Ben Pentreath noticed when he first went to Poundbury and saw the early terraces has not been dispelled: Poundbury remains an uneasy bedfellow to the featureless brick suburbs it abuts. The quality of Poundbury's commercial offer, together with the pleasant streets, open spaces and local shops – obviously a good thing in itself – has meant that businesses from Dorchester have increasingly moved there. Post-Covid, with so many staff from Dorset's big employers – the NHS and the County Council – working from home, it can seem that life has been sucked out of the main town. There is a danger of the tail wagging the dog. But Poundbury has also brought benefits to Dorchester in shared facilities such as schools, the recreation area of the Great Field and a magnificent playground.

And the positives of Poundbury have been noticed by Government. In 2000, a report from the Department of the Environment, Transport and the Regions praised it as an example of the 'anti-Brookside' style of architecture that New Labour wanted to encourage. 'I've seen the past and it works,' said the architectural consultant Francis Golding, one of the authors of the report.[1] (Golding would be killed while riding his bicycle in London in 2013 – sad evidence that the planning utopia he championed had not yet come to pass.) In 2007 the Labour government employed Poundbury's highways engineer Andrew Cameron to help draft the *Manual for Streets*, which succeeded DB32; it praised Poundbury for its winding streets and lanes used by both cars and bicycles: initiatives that had, paradoxically, reduced speeds and traffic accidents.

Poundbury was one of the models that the late Sir Roger Scruton had in mind when, following his appointment to the chair of the Building Better, Building Beautiful Commission in 2018, he and Nicholas Boys Smith reported on ways to improve the delivery of new settlements. It was, he said in a Facebook video,

> a genuine settlement, the proportions are human proportions, the details are restful to the eye. This is not great or original architecture, nor does it try to be – it is a modest attempt to get things right by following patterns and examples laid down by tradition … Architecture that doesn't respect the past is not respecting the present, because it is not respecting people's primary need in architecture, which is to build a long-standing home.

Begun in 1993, Poundbury, as we see it today, is over 30 years old, the product of the hard, innovative thinking that took place a generation ago. That hard thinking has, on Charles's part, continued and the result is not to build more identikit Poundburys. At Truro, where the steeply sloping site did not suit small vernacular homes, Ben Pentreath designed a terrace in the manner of the Royal Crescent at Bath, complete with working chimney pots (the houses have wood burning stoves). The large projects at Nansledan outside Newquay and Faversham in Kent contain many tested ideas but are in other respects Poundbury Mark II and Mark III, advances on the original iteration. Charles's overcoats may suggest the immemorial tailoring of another age but his design philosophy keeps motoring on.

EIGHT

EDEN

Romania

POUNDBURY AND MANY OF CHARLES'S OTHER projects are based on the premise that the world has taken a wrong turn. We ignore the wisdom of our ancestors. Tradition is jettisoned by a society that puts its faith in technology rather than knowledge accumulated over generations. Nature has been put to flight. We have been busily creating dystopias – a nightmare of junk food, obesity, juggernauts, egotism and alienation – whose social consequences will come back to plague us. Not just advanced economies like Britain but the whole planet is now being visited by the existential threat of climate change. So far so bleak, as far as most of Europe and the West are concerned. To use a metaphor from religion, ours is a fallen world. Yet there remain places, even in Europe, which are as God intended, having avoided the heinous consequences of western economic development after the Second World War. Prince Charles found one such Garden of Eden when he went to Romania on an official visit in the late 1990s. It is called Transylvania.

That first time was the only occasion that the Prince went on business. He fell so much under the spell of the place that he bought a house there, in one of the plaster-coated, wattle-and-daub villages, settled, many centuries ago, by Saxons from Germany. Then he acquired another property, which he turned into a comfortable, folksy lodge. Word had it that he has at one point considered the purchase of a third place, perhaps to use as a training workshop to help perpetuate the craft skills that survive in Romania but need encouragement. He makes a private visit every year, if he can, preferably in May when the wildflowers are out. The meadows of Romania are dense with species – as many as six times more to the square metre than are to be found in Britain. The air is fragrant with the scent of herbs. 'Stop!' the Prince once cried when he was walking with friends. 'Here's the Bastard Toadflax. I've wanted to see the Bastard Toadflax for ages.'

You do not have to be in Transylvania for long to realise why Charles was enraptured by it. The country looks as England might have done around the year 1800. There are no fences. Farmers had tractors under Communism but they were abandoned as uneconomical after 1990, leaving horses as a common form of locomotion, not only for road travel but ploughing. The village economy is not, in financial terms, rich; very little money circulates. With poverty goes hardship; a local authority in Britain would regard it as backward and want to reform it as soon as possible. And yet this seemingly primitive existence has compensations, which provide the sense of community and direct contact with Nature which has disappeared across swathes of urban Britain. Almost everything that is needed to support life can be found growing, or is made, in the village. Grapes, sweet from the intense summer sun, cluster from the vines that twine about the eaves of the farmhouses. Geese waddle out of the farmyards. Fruit swells in the orchards. Sheep are guarded by shepherds, often Romani, accompanied by enormous, ferocious dogs, capable of repelling wolves. Beehives are trundled from one location to another,

The gateway of the Blue House in Viscri, giving into the old farmyard. First visiting in 1998, Charles fell in love with a place where craft traditions were still alive and used daily. But the fall of Communism threatened rapid, insensitive change. He encouraged preservationists by buying this farmhouse, which became a guest house and training centre to support conservation, farming and sustainable development. The Prince of Wales's feathers can be seen over the door.

Not long ago, the farmyard would have been full of geese and chickens, while horses and livestock were kept in the barns. It has now been restored with a sensitive hand. The eaves on the right are new.

according to the species of wildflower in bloom, to make the very best honey. It is a land overflowing with good things (you will never taste better jam), where crafts such as weaving and embroidery are still practised. It is hard to find a mega supermarket. Although Romania is part of the European Union, country people do not shop in malls. The towns are far apart, the roads potholed. Life here is local, pastoral and – to Charles's romantic eye – idyllic.

In appearance, the landscape looks something like Shropshire, with more woods and no hedges. Centuries-old trees stand in the meadows, giving shade to cattle in the fierce summer heats. The beechwoods are reminiscent of Sussex; only with hardly anybody about, and no sign of human habitation for miles. Once the sun has gone down, it is easy – in a Hansel and Gretelish manner – to get lost in the immense woods, where tracks are few and signs non-existent. Organic? Yes, inevitably that is the manner of farming here since there is no money for fertilisers, let alone GM seed. 'It's the timelessness' of this prelapsarian world which is 'so important' to Charles. The landscape is 'almost out of some of these stories you used to read as a child. People are yearning for that sense of identity and belonging and meaning.' The simple countryside of Transylvania can still offer it. Richer, more sophisticated countries, such as Britain, must make a tortuous journey to rediscover the spiritual values that were sacrificed to our hedonistic urban lifestyles.

There is no doubting Charles's passion for the natural beauty and sustainable farming that he finds here. To the possible exasperation of some of the Royal Household, Transylvania recharges his batteries as a campaigner for his controversial views about small-scale farming and the vulnerability of the natural world.

We have to rediscover those aspects of the way we produce food, and the way we live with … Nature, if we are to ensure that this whole system continues. That's why human cultural systems matter. Because they're intimately linked to that aspect of Nature. It's in us but we've somehow thrown it away as though it's irrelevant and doesn't matter. But it does matter. *That's* what Romania does for you.

This is a love affair and it is serious.

There are more brown bears in Romania's forests than anywhere else in Europe. They are not shy animals, although when I visited a decade ago I was told they were even more elusive for Charles than the Bastard Toadflax, since he had not actually seen one, even though they have been known to play on the hillside behind his lodge at Zalánpatak (another habitat, as in the US, being urban dustbins). The forests are also home to wolves and lynx.

Charles III's farm at Zalánpatak is surrounded by old-fashioned meadows and the sound of cowbells is heard in the morning and evening. In 2009, Count Kálnoky, whose family won back some of their ancestral lands after the fall of Ceauşescu, turned it into a lodge, rich in craftsmanship and folk art. Log fires and traditional ceramic stoves are the note.

Scientists believe that these large carnivores are essential to the forest ecosystem. Deer, if left unchecked, would eat every young shoot as it appeared above ground. Wolves and lynx control their numbers, making it possible for the forest to regenerate. This has happened in the Highlands of Scotland, to the impoverishment of biodiversity. Paul Lister, who founded The European Nature Trust to campaign for places like the Carpathian Forest, knows this from experience. He owns the Alladale Wilderness Reserve, near Inverness, which he is attempting to 'rewild' by reintroducing some of the animals that would once have roamed the Caledonian Forest. The Carpathians are what Britain has lost. He believes that they should be regarded as Europe's Yellowstone National Park.

Paradoxically, the forests were managed to textbook standards under the Communist regime, not least because the dictator Nicolae Ceauşescu loved to hunt bears in them. Since his fall in 1989, the state forestry service has declined. Large areas of forest have been returned to the families who originally owned them. They might now live far away, and as the price of timber rises, so does the temptation to clear fell for hard cash. Although it might seem hardly possible, given the scale of the operation, which requires the building of new roads to take out the timber, logging can take place illegally. There is no middle class to patrol the activity, as there would be in the UK. Corruption is rife, objectors intimidated and the government tempted to put a greater value on the foreign exchange that can be earned from timber exports than on the sustainability of the forests. The danger to what is an immense natural resource horrify Charles. 'When you pull down swathes of the Carpathian Forest you're destroying one of Nature's great services to mankind in terms of carbon sequestration.'

If even the mighty forests are vulnerable, even more so is the traditional life of the villages. Young Romanians leave for better jobs – some, indeed, to the UK. Old women in headscarves are a familiar sight, as are children. But many of the active generation have gone to improve their prospects overseas. This leaves the Arcadia, which represents everything that developed countries have lost, vulnerable to thoughtless modernisation of the kind that has done so much to wreck the British countryside over the past 100 years. Understandably, many locals want roads which don't break the springs of your car. They do not always see the charm of draughty old houses, which need constant attention, preferring concrete villas with all the modern amenities. Charles would like to persuade them that, instead, Transylvania has something that is precious, which, ultimately, will be more valuable to the people who live there than a land which has been reduced to the globalised norm. At a time when Romanians have become a familiar feature of the British workforce, Charles is leading a small counter-migration: of well-heeled Northern Europeans who delight in species-rich meadows and rickety farmhouses (which, incidentally, can still be bought for a song).

> There's so much we can learn from, it seems to me. It's the last corner of Europe where you see true sustainability and complete resilience, and the maintenance of entire ecosystems to the benefit of mankind and also of Nature. There's so much we can learn from it before it's too late.

There was, sometimes, a note of frustration in the Prince's voice when he found himself fighting a Canute-like battle against an incoming tide of modernity. 'You'd think by now we might have learnt a few lessons from the things that have gone wrong from an agri-industrial approach to everything,' he told the Travel Channel's Charlie Ottley in a series of programmes on *Wild Carpathia* to which he contributed. 'Because the great thing it seems to me about Transylvania is the combination of natural ecosystems – forests and agriculture – together with human cultural systems. It's this extraordinarily unique integrated relationship which is so important.'

Charles's first house is in the village of Viscri. Viscri, although better known than it used to be a few years ago, isn't easy to find, even on a map. It could appear under the old name of Deutschweisskirch (white German church; Viscri is a Romanian corruption of the German and, in this ethnically complicated area, the Hungarian name of Szászfeherégyháza means the same thing). Or it may simply have been left off, deliberately, by the mapmakers. It is one of the Saxon villages, where, until recently, most of the inhabitants – descended from families who had been invited here to defend the border in the Middle Ages – spoke German. Fortified churches doubled as citadels. The Saxons never made themselves popular with their neighbours, and when, with the fall of the Iron Curtain, they saw an opportunity to return to a reunified Germany, up to 90 per cent of them took it. Their old farmhouses were left to crumble. Fortunately, the spirited Jessica Douglas-Home saw the danger and set up the Mihai Eminescu Trust, named after a famous Romanian poet, to rescue them. The one bought by Prince Charles, after a visit in 2002, cost a few thousand pounds.

Even after a decade of gentle improvement, Viscri still gives the impression of having recently emerged from an idealised Middle Ages. There are no pavements, no street lighting, numerous farm animals roaming free. Beyond the reddish tiles of the roof-tops are glimpses of unspoilt countryside, without a wind farm or powerline in sight. A pipe dribbles water into a horse trough. The principal commercial activity consists of village women selling a variety of hand-knitted socks, in striking patterns. The scene could have been set by Zeffirelli. Called the Blue House, after the blue limewash on the façade, against which are set olive green shutters, Charles's property is easily found. Inside, the courtyard, partly cobbled, is planted with vegetables. A vine grows beneath the eaves. The key note is simplicity – which, of course, cannot be preserved without a degree of sophisticated intervention to prevent structures from decaying. To upgrade the farmhouse while retaining the charm of an old village building, Prince Charles recruited Alireza Sagharchi of Stanhope Gate Architects as his architect. Sagharchi preserved a barn by dismantling and rebuilding it. A screen was erected on one of the boundaries to preserve the privacy of the courtyard. The latter, which had previously been open to the village street, was closed with a new wing, and an open loggia was also added. Like many of the Prince's architects, Sagharchi was surprised by the level of detail into which Charles plunged. On visits to Dumfries House, to show samples of wood and materials, Sagharchi found him 'interested in minutiae. He

The library that Alireza Sagharchi of Stanhope Architects made out of a restored barn. The old building, which had been lower than the courtyard, was dismantled and rebuilt a foot higher, so that the footings would be safe from rot. The terracotta floor was made in the Viscri brickworks established by the Prince's Foundation.

understood the plans and studied them thoroughly.' As at Poundbury, drawings sent to Clarence House would come back with copious annotations. 'Depending on what goes on with the neighbouring property this area needs a further extension to mask any ghastly development,' reads one.

Inside, the decoration was arranged by Countess Kálnoky, who with her husband Count Tibor Kálnoky ran the Prince of Wales's charitable foundation in Romania. The theme is of old-fashioned painted chests and time-worn wooden benches. There are only three bedrooms in the main building. The old samplers, locally embroidered towels and hand-woven throws may be ever-so-slightly reminiscent of an artfully rustic *World of Interiors* photo shoot, but the whole is unquestionably delightful. The whole village is. Some of the Saxon families who fled to Germany think it is preferable to the high-rise blocks on the outskirts of industrial cities in which they were housed in the Fatherland, and have started to come back. That the village has survived so beautifully owes much to the imagination and drive of the councillor and former mayor Caroline Fernolend. She talks of the poverty of earlier days, when her father, as a child, was so poor that he shared a pair of shoes with a cousin. It may not be apparent to a casual visitor, but the village is now richer than then – and Charles's example has been followed by more than a dozen affluent incomers, among whom is his neighbour, from Switzerland. He upset the Prince by building an extension to his house that threatened the royal privacy. Welcome to village life, Sir.

At Zalánpatak, Charles found a farmhouse at the end of a lane. He is not troubled by neighbours, and he can walk out directly into the meadows and up into woods. The morning begins

Inside the Blue House, which is simply furnished with traditional furniture and examples of local craftwork, such as handwoven throws and linen curtains. Walls are hung with old carpets that are now too fragile to put on the floor.

with the sound of cowbells, as cattle sway out from their barns into the pasture. The bells are heard again in the evening, as each animal found her way back to her own barn, unaided. Nights velvet-black, their silence only broken by the barking of guard dogs. No ringing of telephones disturbs the tranquillity, not least because the copper wires (on the occasion I was there as a member of the press) had been stolen. Fields of wild crocuses bloom beside the bumpy roads. In summer, hay is heaped up into rum baba-shaped stacks. The designer who, in 2009, turned the farmhouse into this discreetly comfortable, folksy-but-sophicated lodge was Count Kálnoky, whose family won back some of their ancestral lands as part of the restitution programme that followed Ceauşescu's demise – but not enough to make a sufficient income from farming. He is alive, therefore, to the importance of tourism. He also has an eye for the traditional craftsmanship and the folk art beloved of Charles. Between wooden floors and wooden ceilings are white plaster walls. Compared to Highgrove, the Arts and Crafts simplicity is, while not austere, certainly low key. The main cabin, heated by log fires and traditional ceramic stoves, has only three rooms. All the furniture – carved wooden beds, 19th-century chairs, an old oil lamp (converted to electricity) that's suspended from the ceiling, even an ancient radio – has been restored by hand. It's cosy, rustic and tasteful; and definitely not grand.

Some walls are hung with carpets that have become too fragile to use on the floor, although there's a hint of another side of Charles in a drawing of Classical architecture. The old stables have been converted to bedrooms. On the roofs, the intricate jigsaw of pottery tiles has been repaired by skilled workers, for whom the required geometry is almost instinctive. Kálnoky describes the appeal of Zalánpatak as being somewhere that 'the local population lives in total harmony with Nature. It's not a total wilderness, like the mountains, but the perfect cohabitation of man with Nature.'

In 2014, I talked to Maria Grapini, then Romania's Minister for Small and Medium Enterprises, Business Environment and Tourism. She was, naturally, delighted that 'such a huge international personality as Prince Charles' should be singing the beauties of a country that doesn't always enjoy a positive public image. Asked if there is a negative side to his involvement – his inability, for example, to keep his ideas about the environment to himself, which has led him to establish his own secretariat in Romania – she gives an emphatic 'no'. What might be called the Tuscanisation of Transylvania would be a price worth paying if it creates well-paid employment, which will encourage Romanians – in a country whose prime industry is agriculture – to stay on the land. As Count Kálnoky observes: 'Our guest houses employ more people than we have beds.'

Some people of King Charles's age would look forward to spending more time in one of them, as retirement allowed for a leisurely existence in the holiday home. But when I saw the future monarch bounding to the car that would take him to the airport in Bucharest in 2014, he showed no sign of slowing down. Physically, Romania remains a place that he will visit, in a private capacity, for a few days a year – a precious holiday which the King will still cram with visits to enterprises that support his vision of sustainable development. But its importance to him is more than that. Wherever he goes, the memory of it goes with him: a place of the mind, where so many of his most passionately held ideas about humanity's place in the world are played out in everyday life. Not everyone will wear the rose-tinted spectacles to see it, but for those who do, it is a hope-giving example of what might be regained elsewhere.

The year that the Prince bought the Blue House at Viscri, the

Duchy of Cornwall at last managed to find a suitable estate for him to occupy on his visits to Wales. Occupying less than 200 acres of Carmarthenshire, Llwynywermod answered Charles's conviction that he should have at least a toehold in the Principality after which his title was named. There had been a country house here but it was ruined. Rather than rebuild it, Craig Hamilton was asked to convert a nearby farmhouse for royal use. The result was not unlike Viscri and Zalánpatak: everything traditional and local, including wooden plank shutters made from oaks grown on the Duchy estate. The farmyard was torn up and replaced with a garden, planted, as the King likes to say, with his own hands (although those hands may not have done all the preparatory work). The walls of the farmhouse were whitewashed, the woodwork painted a glaucous blue. Dilapidated farm buildings made of concrete and corrugated iron were taken down and replaced by a sheltering range of cottages to create a courtyard, with holiday cottages that could be let out. An old cow byre became a dining room, lit by a window with simplified tracery designed by Hamilton. The abandoned slurry pit was removed, a reed bed filtration system installed. Sombre settles, dressers and Windsor chairs, Welsh blankets, rugs and quilts: the lively hues of the textiles set off the dark tones of the old wooden furniture. The result was 'an air of retired quietude,' to quote the former Editor of *House and Garden*, Sue Crewe, as close to the spirit of Transylvania as it was possible to achieve on the edge of the Brecon Beacons National Park.

Scarcely had the purchase of Llwynywermod been completed in April 2007, when another canvas presented itself. It would be bigger, more challenging and approached in a completely new way. It would use the restoration of an old country estate to give hope, employment and skills to a neglected community, abandoned after the closure of the coal mines that provided its one source of employment. This was Dumfries House.

NINE

RESURRECTION

Dumfries House

O N A SPRING DAY IN 2007, JAMES KNOX, MANAGING director of the *Art Newspaper*, got up to address a conference about conservation at Holyrood House. He was not on the agenda of the meeting but still made an impassioned speech, using the time allotted to questions to do so. As a native of Ayrshire he felt strongly about Dumfries House, which its owner the 7th Marquess of Bute – formerly known as Johnny Dumfries, who had achieved some fame as a racing driver – had decided to sell. Although the last occupant, Bute's grandmother, the Dowager Marchioness, had died in 1993, no heritage solution for the house, contents and estate had been found in the intervening 14 years – in fact, discussion seems not to have opened. For some weeks, Knox had been trying to bring the crisis to public attention. The year before, he had launched a campaign in Scotland to save the house by creating a regeneration strategy which included creating a coal mining museum on the estate. Since then he had joined forces with the tireless campaigner, Marcus Binney of SAVE Britain's Heritage.

The man whose money had built Dumfries House in the 1750s, William Crichton-Dalrymple, 5th Earl of Dumfries, had gone to the best cabinetmaker of the age, Thomas Chippendale, for an astonishing 70 pieces. But with a canny eye on cost, he also had some of Chippendale's designs made up by Scottish craftsmen – also very fine but considerably cheaper. Not a stick of furniture had been taken out of the house in nearly 300 years, making Dumfries House a unique repository of the best 18th-century Rococo furnishings, in which the documented Scottish pieces had become even rarer than those by Chippendale himself. The house had come to the Butes in the 19th century. 'It would have been a catastrophe to have dispersed the collection,' says Knox. 'What's more, Dumfries House offered such an immense opportunity for regeneration.' At the centre of an estate of over 2,000 acres, Dumfries House lies in the bleak former coalfields of East Ayrshire, whose principal employer – the deep coal mines – closed in the 1980s. By 2007, some local families were in the third generation of unemployment. The villages were so devoid of opportunity that, at a time when the rest of the country was wracking its brains where to build houses, the council had been knocking perfectly good dwellings down because there was zero demand for them. But at Holyrood House, Knox found himself apparently speaking to deaf ears.

> Having said my piece, I sat down to stony silence. The heritage establishment wasn't interested. They wanted whatever money was in the system to go to other projects. I was in despair.

But there was one person in the room who had heard and understood his message. By chance, Knox's seat was behind that of the Prince of Wales.

> After I had spoken, the Prince's equerry turned to me and said I should follow the Prince out of the room. I did so. He was interested.

Unsurprisingly, given his critique of the carbuncle and his attachment to the fabric of the City of London shown in his Mansion
House speech, Charles had always been as concerned about the
fate of old architecture as he was about the form of the new. This
was the heroic age of architectural conservation, with SAVE
Britain's Heritage leading the preservationist charge. Under its
founder Marcus Binney, SAVE's approach was more innovative
than that of the old-fashioned heritage establishment which had
previously turned a deaf ear to the pleas on behalf of Dumfries
House. It pioneered a new way of seeing old buildings: the example
of America and, in this country, Kit Martin had shown that they
could be an asset as much as a liability. Binney had both the
imagination to find new, income-generating uses for what other
people only saw as lost causes and the energy to champion his
ideas in the press: campaigns were all-consuming and very vocal.
He also had a hotline to the Prince – although he was both too
much of a diplomat and a master strategist to overplay it. His
advocacy for derelict textile mills and other immense buildings,
often Victorian, their potential often invisible to the communities
in which they stood, captured Charles's imagination; he established
the Phoenix Trust as a revolving fund, whereby the money raised
to convert one structure to a profitable new use would be returned
to the fund once the project was successfully completed, so that
it could be used to rescue another case. Revolving funds had been
established before but not on the scale needed for, say, a row of
19th-century factory buildings on the scale of Stanley Mills, north
of Perth: an immense complex of derelict water-powered mills on
the River Tay, which the Trust helped to rescue and convert to
apartments from 1997. With Knox, Binney proposed a twofold
solution for Dumfries House, which included both a museum of
coal mining that would turn the negatives of the industrial legacy
into a positive, and a property development à la Poundbury on

the edges of the estate. Two weeks after Knox had met Charles at Holyrood, he went with Binney to Clarence House. It sealed Charles's determination to help. 'When we were leaving,' says Knox, 'the Prince said he was going to make some phone calls. Next day I got a call to say those calls had raised £20 million in promises.'

Even so it was not enough: Bute wanted £45 million for the house and estate. Knox and Binney had named a target of £25 million to the Prince because the full amount seemed unattainable. But Charles's money gave them a magnificent boost. They could leverage it by appealing to the National Heritage Memorial Fund, the Monument Trust and the Warburg Charitable Trust; this brought in almost another £5 million. And yet there was still what seemed like an unfilled and unfillable chasm of £20 million. The clock was ticking. The furniture lorries were at the doors of Dumfries House and being loaded with Chippendale. But at the last moment Charles managed to do something that probably no Prince of Wales before him had so much as considered: he persuaded the Duchy Council that he should get a loan. This was done through the Prince's Foundation. Collateral was provided by the prospect of a small housing development at New Cumnock, the nearby town. Designed by Ben Pentreath, this was known officially as Knockroon, although inevitably dubbed McPoundbury by critics. Even sympathisers thought that the project – saving and restoring a country house in such an unpromising location and paying for it with houses which nobody might buy – showed the unworldly side of the Prince's nature. 'Bonkers' was one of the kinder words used. Certainly it involved a degree of commercial risk alien to the bean counters of HM Treasury, which oversees the Duchy of Cornwall. But the Prince managed it, and in the nick of time. As Charles would later recall,

Furniture vans were already taking the Chippendale furniture and other contents from Dumfries House in Ayrshire, to be auctioned in London when Prince Charles succeeded in halting the sale in 2007. Since then, not only have the house and collection been restored but the estate has been made the centre of numerous training initiatives in the crafts, hospitality and agriculture, providing hope for a community that had suffered multi-generational unemployment since the closure of local coal mines in the 1980s.

By the time the negotiations and all the horrors of putting the money together were finally concluded, there were three huge pantechnicons already laden with furniture with labels on all going down to London.

The lorries were stopped at 1pm on the motorway somewhere in Cumbria, and turned around.

When those events in 2007 were soon followed by a financial crisis and property crash, it might have seemed to those Treasury officials that they had been right. Given the state of the market, Knockroon was not an instant hit. Even so, the

Cassandras counted without the palpable love that Charles developed for his new project. He delighted in getting this once-crumbling estate back on its feet, in such a way as to make Dumfries House a motor of regeneration for the entire community. More than 100 local jobs have been created as a result. From the start, he would visit regularly and soon made it his base of operations during the week he spends on official business in Scotland each year. Previously, like the Queen before him, the Prince had stayed at Holyrood House. Changing his place of residence to Dumfries House showed his faith in the local community. He would leave his usual staff behind, preferring to be served by youngsters from the local towns and villages. Scottish ministers and other bigwigs who wanted to see him had to visit this ravaged part of the world, where previously they might never have set foot.

Remarkably, Charles himself had not visited Dumfries House before it was acquired by his Foundation. 'I'd never actually seen the house, but I'd seen photos,' Charles told a newspaper. 'I knew it was important and should be preserved for the nation. It's so unusual to have a house with all its original furniture in it.' Had he been through the doors, he might not have liked it. Like many homes inhabited by the very old it had become forlorn and shabby. The Dowager Marchioness was a colourful character who allowed her labradors to lounge on the Rococo furniture; burns in the precious Axminster carpets were evidence of her 80-a-day cigarette habit. Yes, there were the chairs, looking glasses, tables and beds, but would people without Charles's aesthetic interests really come all the way to Ayrshire to see what auctioneers disparagingly call 'brown furniture' – unfashionable these days, despite its fine lineage? The park seemed even sorrier than the house: little maintenance had been done since the Arts and Crafts architect Robert Weir Schultz had sympathetically extended the house and

The King's Foundation has turned Dumfries House into a centre for the training of young people in hospitality, gardening, agriculture and the crafts. Here students are seen practising skills in stained glass and wrought iron.

designed garden architecture in the 1890s. Outbuildings lay in ruins and the rotting stonework on the elegant bridge designed by Robert Adam's brother John was in a dreadful state. Local youths had kicked one baluster after another into the river below. It would have taken a visionary to predict that the house could ever be more than a white elephant; it might appeal to the posh, like Prince Charles and his friends, but not to the people. And the posh did not often go to Cumnock.

Under the newly formed Great Steward of Scotland's Dumfries House Trust (the property was later transferred to the Prince's Foundation) the transformation has been nothing short of amazing. Every piece of furniture in the house has been revived using the best restorers in Scotland. With new upholstery, using sumptuously coloured silks sometimes specially woven from existing fragments, the rooms sing. The Georgian four-poster beds are spectacular. Delicate wall decorations have been found beneath layers of cream paint. Portraits on loan from the National Galleries of Scotland and the Fleming Collection hang on the walls. It is easy to see why Charles enjoys staying and entertaining here. It has become what it must have been when Lord Dumfries built it with the aim of attracting a new wife: an extraordinarily glamorous dwelling. Although grand, the rooms are not enormously big, but must be just right for the sort of dinner parties that Charles most enjoys, where a choice group of influential people are nudged towards supporting his causes.

Strangely, the figures stack up better than doubters would have thought. Let's look first at the purchase price. The Earl of Dumfries who paid £4 10s each for a set of 14 Chippendale chairs would be justified in congratulating himself on his investment. The King, however, might do the same since similar chairs can sell for nearly £1.5 million at auction. Dumfries contains a valuable example of early Chippendale in the form of a bookcase:

that alone is valued at up to £20 million, despite an 18th-century crack in one of its glass door panels. And although Knockroon, the housing development, got off to a slow start following the collapse of the property market in 2008, the first streets have been built and sold, and look – well, exactly like traditional architecture of the Regency period, which is just what His Majesty would like. Suddenly, the £20 million loan guaranteed by the Prince seems less reckless. He has also been able to reduce his exposure by raising sponsorship money from wealthy donors and perhaps without those funds, the good ship *Dumfries House* would founder, given the extent, and cost, of the charitable activities being carried out there. But business in the House itself is undoubtedly brisk. Visitors have to move quickly before the next clients roll in. A wedding at lunchtime is followed by an evening function, with another planned for lunchtime the next day. Despite its depressed location, this venue is practically fully booked the year round.

The House, though, is only part of the project – the centre-piece, yes, but not the main action. That lies in the activities taking place around the estate, many of them run by other charities such as the Prince's Trust. 'One of the main reasons I thought it was worth taking this appalling risk,' Prince Charles reflected,

> was that I could try to make a difference to the local area at the same time as saving the house. I'm one of those people who rather likes taking on the most difficult challenges. I'm absolutely convinced that through heritage-led regeneration, you can achieve an awful lot. How do you raise people's aspi-rations, build their self-esteem and develop the necessary skills to substitute for previous traditional industries? These are all things I feel are of huge importance. I wanted to show that

this place could produce some of the best skilled young people in the country. This is what we're trying to do.

When I spoke to Thomas Breckney, then a collections assistant in the house, he said his life has been turned around.

I come from a traditional mining family. When the mines closed down, unemployment became a way of life. For [Charles] to bring in a project like this has not only created jobs but also training opportunities where people can take skills out into the community and get jobs elsewhere. From the perspective of an area that was lost, what he's done has been quite fantastic.

The cookery and catering school provides a place for local young-sters to learn a skill and, for the first time in a generation, give them hope. Chef Darren Blunden chooses a dozen youngsters who have left school with no qualifications to become his appren-tices for blocks of five weeks at a time. By the time they leave, the young trainees are in a far better position to find jobs. Quite a few of have been offered employment by the Royal Household and are now working at Buckingham Palace and other royal establishments.

In the stonemasons' yard, local people get the chance to become craftsmen, also in dry stone walling and woodworking, with a focus on conservation. The bridge that was falling down is now sparkling. Gazebos around the estate, made by the apprentices, are decorated with carved inscriptions and stone heraldic motifs. A newly planted arboretum leads to the Queen Elizabeth II Walled Garden. One side is lined with new glasshouses, of the kind beloved of the Victorian age. Usually, country-house glasshouses are falling down, not freshly built. Below them, going down to the river, are flower beds and the vegetable garden that grows much of the organic produce used by the burgeoning catering operation in the cafes and house. Children are encouraged to grow vegetables, play in the gardens and walk their dogs. The promise of the garden designer Michael Innes to 'recreate the original productive spirit of the place' and generate 'an abundance of joy' has been fulfilled. Elsewhere, a Chinese footbridge inspired by a design by Weir Schultz has been made from wood on stone footings, as an alternative to the Adam bridge over the River Lugar.

On my visits I have never been able to find the engineering workshop, intended, in Charles's words, 'to bring great awareness to the possibilities and potential' of manufacturing. I can, however, testify to the comfort of the luxury B&B (there is also a more basic bunkhouse) which provides visitor accommodation in an area where previously nobody much had reason to linger. 'I do think it is beginning to achieve what I had originally planned,' Charles had been quoted as saying.

> Just by getting things done on the estate, bringing the house back to life, starting to build different new things and do up buildings, using them for skills training and all the things that I wanted to do – bit by bit, the atmosphere, that feeling or whatever, begins to spread locally. Hopefully, it gradually starts to feed into rising levels of self-confidence.

The latest initiative is a rural skills training centre to teach about farm-based jobs.

When the King is in residence at Dumfries (locals drop the 'House') the place becomes a whirl of activity – literally so, when he helicopters off to his official engagements. It remains almost as busy with projects when its royal patron is absent. Textile conservators and specialists run a studio for lace-making and

Inside a covered bridge made of green oak at Dumfries House. In the medieval manner, the dramatic frame of arched trusses is held together by oak pegs rather than screws or nails. It is the work of Jonny Briggs, who received a nine-month Building Craft Apprenticeship from the Prince's Foundation in 2011 to learn heritage skills such as timber framing.

textile conservation attended by 1,300 pupils a year. This is in keeping with Dumfries's history: one of Weir Schultz's additions was a sumptuous tapestry room, lined with cedar to repel moths and hung with four superb tapestries dating to around 1700. They were given to Lord Dumfries's uncle, Lord Stair, by Louis XIV when Lord Stair was ambassador in Versailles.

At the start of the Dumfries project, a local paper ran the headline 'CHARLIE IS THEIR DARLING'. Folk who felt that the world had forgotten them were deeply moved to discover that a very high-profile individual had their interests at heart. The vandalism that used to plague the estate has stopped. People recognise that at last somebody is on their side. Outside the park not only Cumnock but neighbouring New Cumnock have

This ten-sided woodland shelter sits amid the arboretum at Dumfries House. It was designed by building craft apprentices at the Prince's Foundation Summer School in 2013 and erected under the guidance of the oak-framer Jonny Briggs and other tutors. The programme gives aspiring craftspeople the chance to learn through work on real projects.

been revitalised and the long-derelict town hall revived as a community space and an outdoor swimming pool restored to Art Deco splendour.

One of the most astonishing aspects of the Dumfries House project is the political alchemy that surrounds it. Scotland's then First Minister Alex Salmond was a supporter, having been instrumental in positioning the Scottish Executive to support the purchase of Dumfries House with a contribution of £5 million. All manner of Scottish notables and planning gurus have been to see Poundbury and come back reportedly goggle-eyed. According to the *Ayrshire Post*, Charles won over 'a community nurtured by working class heroes' such as the one-time Secretary of the Ayrshire Miners' Association and resident of Cumnock, Keir Hardie. His involvement has given new hope to a community that has felt itself to be on the scrap heap and forgotten for a quarter of a century. As the late Hank Dittmar, Chief Executive of the Prince's Foundation, once put it to me, 'People there keep saying, "We can't believe this has happened to us. Life isn't a Walt Disney movie."' But on this occasion, it is.

TEN

GREEN

Tregunnel Hill and Nansledan

E VER SINCE THE 'CARBUNCLE' SPEECH IN 1984, Prince Charles had been associated in the public mind with a certain attitude to architecture – a preoccupation with style. He had been cast as a Classicist. There was some justice in that: he encouraged John Simpson's counter-scheme at Paternoster Square and, through the Duchy of Cornwall, commissioned work at Poundbury from, seemingly, every Classical architect he had ever met. But this is only part of the story. We have seen, for example, that Charles is as attracted by traditional building techniques, sacred geometry and fanciful follies as he is by the grandeur of Classicism; and all his interests are subservient to his overarching search for Harmony. Besides, the ideas evolved as Charles's experience broadened and new global priorities emerged. This can be seen from the Duchy of Cornwall's developments outside the Cornish coastal town of Newquay, begun some 20 years after Poundbury had got going.

Poundbury was at times so fizzing with ideas that it seemed over-busy. Nansledan would be happier in its own skin. Mere appearance would take a back seat, and the emphasis would now be on place. In an area of low incomes and seasonal employment, supporting the local economy is as important as the character of the streetscape. Sustainability, always a pressing concern for Charles, would occupy an even more important place in the scheme of things than it did at Poundbury. Again, this is met by the local agenda: building materials that come from nearby have fewer miles to travel to the place of construction than those that are industrially produced elsewhere. And, as it happens, they look better too.

Of course, Poundbury was not only about traditional architecture, so viscerally loathed by the architectural establishment for its back-to-the-future vibe. It also pioneered the concept of 'walkability' (the priority of pedestrians over the car) and mixed use (the idea that workspaces could be built near people's homes). Affordable homes are scattered among the more expensive properties; visually, there is nothing to tell them apart. All these ideas are hard-wired into Nansledan. But the Cornish development goes to another level in terms of sustainability and localism.

Tim Gray, the Duchy of Cornwall's estate surveyor and chief of operations at Nansledan, articulated ideas that echo Charles's.

How society chooses to house people is every bit as important as how it chooses to feed people. If you can get those two things right you will be both happier, healthier, better able to engage socially so as to be a contributor as opposed to a burden on the state and the planet. At Nansledan the ambition to build community, to engender civic pride, to secure it through the Design and Community Code, to be liveable so that you can meet your daily needs conveniently on foot, not to differentiate between homes of different tenures and to be connected socially and positively with the adjacent settlements should

A bright day in Nansledan, the Duchy of Cornwall's model development outside Newquay in Cornwall, whose architecture and colours reflect the vernacular of Cornwall's seaside towns.

At a time when high streets elsewhere in Britain are under pressure, the Duchy of Cornwall is bravely creating new ones. They are flourishing. Local shops are an element of the local food strategy which supports employment in the area and reduces food miles. The building work that can be seen at the end of the street will provide more homes and therefore more customers.

provide good foundations for the debate that lies ahead in deciding how the nation should be building homes in the future. There really is an alternative.

We know that Charles visited Nansledan on July 16, 2014, because a plaque there says so. He used to return every year as Prince of Wales, causing the heart of its master planner, Hugh Petter, to beat a little faster as his work was put under the spotlight. Tall and rubicund, Petter could have walked out of a portrait by Gainsborough – a captain in Nelson's navy, perhaps. In fact, he is a partner in ADAM Architecture, based in Winchester and said to be the largest firm of traditional architects in Europe. One of his jobs was to show Charles an Art Deco seahorse that had just been fixed to a building called Chi Morvargh (Cornish for Seahorse Building) as one of the project's decorative flourishes. Art Deco seemed as though it could have been a bit of a walk on the wild side for the architecturally conservative Prince of Wales. In truth, though, Petter rested easy. The detail did not come as a surprise, having, like everything at Nansledan, been personally approved by The Boss, who would insist on seeing each drawing, sample and idea at Clarence House. Charles may have been a busy man but nothing was too small to escape his attention; he took a close interest in the paint colours, for example. Like the seahorse, they are bright and cheerful, in a Cornish, seasidy sort of way – which could be a bit strong for some tastes. 'Make them bolder,' he said. Anyone who has seen the delphiniums in his garden at Highgrove will know he is not afraid of vivid hues.

Art Deco and jaunty colours can be found in almost any holiday resort in the vicinity. Even more specifically Cornish are the street names – Gwarak Agravayn, Bownder Marhaus and Stret Morgan Le Fay. To get them right, the Nansledan team has been working with MAGA Cornish Language Partnership. They reflect local field names, as well as tales of Arthurian romance (Tintagel, where King Arthur was supposedly conceived, is 30 miles away). Nansledan is itself a Cornish word meaning broad valley. Names are carved into tablets of Delabole slate, again from Cornwall. The kerbs of the street are edged with Cornish granite, from a nearby quarry that has been given a new lease of life. The quarry provides local jobs, and so do the builders responsible for the work – C.G. Fry & Son, Morrish Builders and Wain Homes: chosen, in the case of the first two, as firms from the South-West, well known to the Duchy, whose work not only requires local labour but helps to establish local supply chains. They form what Gray calls a 'consortium' with the Duchy, a method that ensures the architecture is practical and appropriate for the local market, while remaining 'HRH-friendly'.

It may be that we do not hear so much about localism now as in the heyday of the Localism Act, 2011; but it is part of Nansledan, the whole idea of which is to meet local need. This alone would make it different from Poundbury, located outside the reasonably prosperous county town of Dorchester; although Poundbury was conceived as a birth-to-death sort of place, with house sizes to suit people of every age, it has at times seemed to attract more than its share of retirees – the West Country being a magnet for the silver-haired. Newquay has a quite different demographic. Quite apart from its reputation as being the Teenage Love Capital of Europe, the destination of many a boy or girl who has just finished A-levels or GCSEs, it is poor and homes are particularly needed by young people. And that demographic seems to like what it sees, from the number of 20- and 30-somethings and young families who are out on the streets. At Tregunnel Hill, the trial development that preceded the larger Nansledan, the initial population of residents was about 80 per

Decorative roof finials are just one of the many details in the project's pattern book that contribute to Nansledan's overall aesthetic. Jaunty colours throughout the town offer the visual equivalent of a blast of ozone. An espaliered pear tree like this one creates a personal relationship with food. Wildlife is also encouraged, with nearly 1,000 built-in nest boxes aimed at endangered species such as swifts, while also providing homes for sparrows, starlings, and house martins.

cent local. That figure falls to two-thirds at Nansledan but, according to Gray, that may not be a wholly bad thing: 'We want to attract some young people from up country because they bring new ideas.'

Wherever they come from, Nansledan reflects the values often shared by the young. 'They have an appetite for a really wholesome lifestyle. Building a community is a really important part of that.' Like California, Cornwall is lifestyle-focused, with a greater openness to the green agenda than some metropolitan areas. So they do not find anything odd about the Prince's much lampooned 'holistic' approach; on the contrary, it is just what they are after. Outsiders may mock the edible gardens (herbs and fruit bushes are planted next to houses), espaliered pear trees and bee bricks (bricks with holes that are laid into the eaves of houses to welcome threatened bee populations), but they go down well here; they are also the outward and visible expression of a consistent philosophy. As well as local style, local materials and local employment … local food.

This is symbolised by the community orchard. Next to it, the Duchy has given seven acres of land that has been energetically – and, when I visited, back-breakingly – turned into allotments. 'Trespassers will be composted,' reads one of the signs that personalise it. Orchard and allotments are among the more conspicuous features of a local food web formulated in a 54-page food strategy document, published on the Nansledan website. With something approaching a quarter of Britain's greenhouse gas emissions being produced by the food industry, anything that can be done to reduce food miles – and to educate children about healthy eating – must be good. At Nansledan, however, the community orchard and allotments fulfil another function: placed on the edge of the new development, they are somewhere that people from Nansledan meet long-time Newquay residents. 'Place-making' is the buzzword among thoughtful planners, but Nansledan is a rare example where it is done well.

Nansledan and Tregunnel Hill feel calmer than Poundbury. The houses and small apartment blocks are less fussy. A particularly prominent building – perhaps on a junction or at the end of a view – may be given extra emphasis, by means of a Classical porch or slate-hung façade; and some fun has been had with monuments, such as the obelisk which is justified as a traffic calming measure. But the feel generally is understated, and much more akin to a genuine vernacular than the at times frenetic incident of Poundbury. Besides, whereas Poundbury is flat, Nansledan and Tregunnel Hill have more ups and downs; the topography lends a natural variety. Something over 4,000 homes will be built.

As the development progresses, buyers are willing to pay a significant premium over equivalent new homes elsewhere. That is hardly surprising, given that Nansledan has so much more to offer than a standard housing estate, whose developer moves on as soon as he has built and sold the properties. The Duchy of Cornwall takes the long view. It will not hurry the pace; less than 100 houses come onto the market in any year. No faster rate is possible because of the limited supply of the building skills involved. As a result, it will take decades for the whole site to be built out – a timescale that is inconceivable to volume house builders like Persimmon. This, however, is central to the Duchy model. While it invests heavily in the early years, it knows – because Poundbury has confirmed this – that the value of its land will go up, and it will more than recoup the initial expenditure through later sales. The key is that it already owns the land.

The whole problem of Britain's housing industry is land. So little of it is available for building that developers fight to get hold of whatever they can, at whatever the price. There's little money left for place-making. Charles's model isn't right every-where, but is already appealing to other estates such as Burghley and Blenheim. It could work for local authorities, pension funds and other bodies that own land. If that happened, future historians wouldn't look back on Nansledan as the Prince of Wales's seaside caprice (in the spirit of an earlier Prince of Wales's Brighton Pavilion) but as the beginning of a movement which made Britain better to live in.

Around 2010, politicians such as Gordon Brown promoted 'Eco Towns' as a solution to the housing crisis. Sceptics presumed that this would be no more than a passing fad and so it proved; the idea did not gain traction. Almost certainly the 'eco' element would have been window dressing. This has not been the case at Tregunnel Hill and Nansledan. The intention is to make them as sustainable as it is possible to be. Expectations in this regard have risen even in the decade since Poundbury was started. Tregunnel Hill could be powered by renewable energy (depending on plan-ning permission); there will be strategies to minimise water use, and increase composting; allow water to soak naturally back into the ground through permeable paving and courtyard soakaways; and encourage the consumption of local food. 'Carbon neutrality as a mantra used by government does not take account of the food people eat, which accounts for 23 per cent of their carbon footprint,' says Gray.

Whereas the reception given to Eco Towns by their neighbours was generally less than warm, the Duchy's patient process of public consultation – known by the catch phrase 'Enquiry-by-Design' – has ensured that its proposals are popular with Newquay's existing population. The rate of building may seem agonisingly slow to a Prime Minister anxious to bless the country with millions of new homes, but it suits a landed estate such as the Duchy which can afford to take a long view and husband its asset. The

Kite flying and dog walking: two of the activities for which the open space is used at Nansledan. The local demographic has made it popular with young families.

last thing they would want to do is to push too many houses onto the market at once, thereby depressing prices. The Duchy may be green, but it is not stupid. They saw at Poundbury that what other developers might regard as expensive extras – public buildings, high-quality architecture – enabled them to sell at a premium. They will want the same effect to happen at Newquay. But 40 per cent of the development will provide affordable housing.

What of the vexed subject of architecture? Petter has drawn up a detailed pattern book and design manual of the Cornish vernacular, showing the sort of design features that house builders might adopt. In addition, they will be constrained to fit in with a masterplan, specifying a hierarchy of different sizes of house, according to the visual importance of the street. So far, so Poundbury. The new aspect of Tregunnel Hill is the contribution that this approach to design, based on local materials such as granite and slate, will help the Cornish economy. The slate does not come from Brazil, nor the granite from China. Thus, design will contribute to the sustainability of the whole project. There are altogether seven aspects of the Sustainability Strategy that the Duchy has devised in conjunction with Restormel Borough Council, each set out in a booklet published on the Duchy's website.

Have Tregunnel Hill and Nansledan been a success? Yes, for four reasons. First, the local authority is so confident of the approach that it has made Nansledan the subject of a Local Development Order. This in effect gives outline planning permission to the entire development. The LDO not only simplifies the process of getting planning permission, thereby reducing the Duchy's costs. It also helps in attracting new businesses, who need not fear that the premises they need will be held up in planning. Generally, LDOs can be a planning carrot that helps to promote good design: there are major benefits to the developer in obtaining one, although Council retains a stick with which to beat malefactors – it has the right to withdraw an LDO if the developer abuses his privileged position. We can expect to see them used more across the country. Nansledan was one of the first. Once again the Duchy has led the way.

Second, government is clearly happy with the way things have gone. Photographs of Nansledan have been used on the covers of the 2020 White Paper *Planning for the Future*, the 2021 *National Model Design Code* and other documents. Here and elsewhere, it is held up as an example of best practice in place-making. Third, in 2021 the RIBA gave Nansledan one of its awards, 'internationally regarded as a mark of excellence'. As Petter comments, 'that would never have happened 20 years ago.' The lion has lain down with the lamb. Fourth, as a community Nansledan works – witness the popularity of local shops. These small businesses are bustling. Elsewhere in Britain, high streets are in a state of crisis. At Nansledan, a new one has been built. And because life here is local, it does well. Clearly Charles has got something right.

ELEVEN

LEGACY

NOT LONG BEFORE HE WAS CROWNED, THE KING invited favourite architects to tea at Windsor Castle. Afterwards he took his guests into the Royal Library where he showed them drawings by Palladio, Leonardo and Holbein. It was the stuff of fables, a glimpse of the extraordinary treasures of the Royal Collection made possible by the kind intentions of His Majesty, not just a King but a warm and thoughtful human being.

We might also see it as a rite of passage. A phase of Charles's life – a long one – was over, now that the main purpose for which he was born had begun. He was telling the architects that he had moved into a different space. Most people's legacy is not judged until they are dead. It is not like that for the King. As regards architecture, he can no longer be the boldly outspoken player that he was in his Prince of Wales years. True, he could encourage the Duchy of Lancaster, his private estate as monarch, to explore Poundbury-like options for its 45,000 acres of land, but it would take time for these to get going. Meanwhile, we can take stock. It is time to rate his achievement.

At the most basic level, as I hope this book will have shown, there is a lot to it. Charles's engagement with architecture was not limited to a few speeches or projects. He was engaged over a broad front during the best part of 40 years. He defeated the carbuncle; championed John Simpson's Paternoster Square scheme; offered for some years a different kind of education for would-be architects; promoted hand drawing and sacred geometry; pioneered new principles of development at Poundbury and Nansledan; helped to regenerate former industrial sites through the Phoenix Trust; rescued Dumfries House and its contents, turning them into a centre for the training of young people in a deprived area; celebrated and encouraged the traditional crafts of Romania; and made Highgrove House and its estate into a personal Arcadia which provides a demonstration of his beliefs. Among the themes that he has consistently pursued over the decades are community, sustainability, the crafts, education, youth employment, traditional building methods, Classicism, patterns in Nature, and his overarching idea of Harmony. He has wanted to make the world a more attractive place for ordinary people to live in. Surely a big canvas.

Equally, after decades in the wilderness, the planning ideas that were pioneered at Poundbury and developed at Nansledan and other Duchy sites have entered the mainstream. Neighbourhoods where shops and services are accessible by foot; where workplaces are mixed in with residential accommodation; whose carbon footprint is low; where affordable housing stands cheek by jowl with dwellings sold at market rates, from which it is not visibly different, rather than being crammed onto the worst part of the site as a ghetto; whose character is determined by local materials; which are as sustainable as possible, and bolster the local economy; which encourage human interaction, in attractively designed public spaces – 30 years ago, it was radical to propose such communities. Now many of the ideas Charles championed as Prince have been adopted as public policy. Alas, ambitions are one thing, bringing them to fruition is another, not least because the toothless planning system can do no more than snap at well-funded developers. Poundbury and Nansledan remain rare demonstrations of the principles having been put into practice. So they deserve all the more study. At a time of acute housing shortage, good masterplanning should help to reduce the local opposition that prevents new developments from being built. For example, Nansledan has grown from 400 to 4,000 homes because the community liked what it saw and wanted more of it. Has this happened anywhere else?

The Duchy's prowess as a developer has been recognised at Faversham, where Swale Borough Council specifically invited it to offer development proposals for land to the south-east of the town in order to help address the local housing shortage. Environmentally the thinking behind South-East Faversham is an advance even on Nansledan. 'It starts with the soil, the trees and the water,' says the landscape architect Kim Wilkie, who with Ben Pentreath is the masterplanner. 'This means that everything emerges together, rather than being treated as isolated elements.' The hope is not merely to maintain the quality of the ecology and landscape – which is not so hard because the fields are intensively farmed and have little biodiversity at present – but, over time, to improve it.

Given that billions more people will soon be alive on the planet, the need to build more homes is not an issue for the UK alone. Many countries will have to create new cities, whose inhabitants – if those cities are to work properly – ought to feel happy where they live. It is in the interest of the whole world to avoid slums and shanty towns which breed lawlessness, extremism and discontent. As a result, the Duchy of Cornwall's methods are increasingly studied, not only in this country but abroad.

While extensive, Charles's legacy in architecture is diffuse. According to Ben Pentreath, 'This is somebody who is operating in a million different fields and perspectives and who possesses both an astonishing generality of interests and an equally astonishing depth of focus.' He likens his mind to

> the beam of a lighthouse as it revolves very slowly. For a brief minute, very intermittently you or your project or your situation is in full glare. And then there is quite a long period where you are back in darkness … When you are in the glare, you feel that the spotlight is really on you – he needs to know what's happening, why it is happening like this, rather than this, or whatever; but you also feel quite loved or adored.

The lighthouse analogy illustrates the multiplicity of Charles's enthusiasms, each pursued with a tenacity remarkable for someone with so many diary commitments. As a result, his legacy resembles a more or less planned landscape made up of numerous different features rather than a single monument.

This is demonstrated by the organisation formed to contain the architectural causes closest to his heart when he had to part from them on becoming monarch. The King's Foundation is one of two charities, the other being the King's Trust, created during the new reign and bearing the King's name. Formed out of the Prince's Foundation, itself the successor to the Prince of Wales's Foundation for the Built Environment (later for Building Community), it is the ultimate heir to the Prince of Wales's Institute of Architecture, whose eight lively and chaotic years of existence from 1993 to 2001 were described earlier in the book.

The changes of name reflect a storm-tossed history, from which the Foundation has emerged as (to borrow Henry James's phrase) something of a 'large, loose, baggy monster', containing several initiatives that we have already encountered – including the School of Traditional Arts (the successor to VITA) as well as Dumfries

House and its many activities. It is at Dumfries House that the King's Foundation is based.

The King's Foundation is not only a conventional charity which offers educational courses while preserving a major cultural asset. It also plays an active role in town planning. Projects have included an urban extension of over 100 acres at Upton, outside Northampton; the regeneration of a former oil refinery at Coed Darcy in Wales as a settlement of 4,000 new homes; and Sherford, a new town on a 1,200-acre site outside Plymouth. These and other projects showcased Enquiry-by-Design, a fruit of Charles's interest in Community Architecture. During the New Labour years, the Prince's Foundation came to the attention of no less a potentate than the Deputy Prime Minister John Prescott, who poached its chief executive to become his director of Urban Policy. As a result, Enquiry-by-Design is now enshrined in national planning guidance. Meanwhile, the King's Foundation hired out its services, providing masterplanning expertise in the hope of improving the standard of development, with the profits going back into the Foundation.

Such initiatives show a legacy that goes beyond the many projects in which Charles himself was closely concerned. Through the King's Foundation they have a longevity that continues into the new reign and will no doubt outlast it. Not every project – for reasons that have nothing to do with the input from Charles's organisation – fulfils its promise: masterplanned by the Prince's Foundation, Sherford was built out by Taylor Wimpey and other volume house builders, whose commercial model meant that much of the Poundbury-style value-added content was dropped.

There is also Building a Legacy, the name given to a movement, as yet largely among estate owners, to replicate the Poundbury idea. Given the housing shortage, many estates are being pressed to develop their land and it is in their commercial interest to do so. Conventionally, they would have done this simply by selling development land to a volume house builder, with the usual banausic results. Volume house builders, having paid a high price for the land, have nothing left to spend on infrastructure or amenities, let alone architecture. But at a time of undersupply everything sells and a quick return is made to their shareholders. Landed estates, as the Duchy of Cornwall has shown, are in a different position. They already own the land. They can be patient and wait for the higher return that comes from better development and place-making on the Poundbury model. Higher investment in the early years means that the value of the land rises as the development is built out. Besides, the families who own big estates expect to be there for the foreseeable future and beyond – they will not want to create a horror at the gateway to their own country house. They and their successors will have to live with the consequences in perpetuity. Over a dozen estates have now joined the club including Blenheim, Burghley, Englefield and Wilton. To date, the largest such development is Tornagrain, a new town of 5,000 homes east of Inverness, masterplanned by Andrés Duany and DPZ, which was granted outline approval in the summer of 2012. Ben Pentreath has been designing the houses.

Building a Legacy is not the answer to all Britain's housing needs but can make a significant contribution – perhaps a tenth of the requirement. The hope is that other kinds of investors such as pension funds, institutional landowners like the Church Commissioners and Crown Estate, universities, the Ministry of Defence and the NHS will follow suit.

By such means Charles has leveraged the success of Poundbury and Nansledan and spread the joy to some unexpected places – Thurrock, for example, where his Foundation contributed towards the evolution of the local plan. And further even than that. A look at Charles's collected speeches shows that many of them were given overseas. These were often major events for those who heard them. We have seen the success of his Urban Task Forces in the 1990s, working from Potsdam in German to Sidon in Lebanon. Those are not the only projects across the globe that show his influence. Rose Town, Jamaica, was in a worse state even than Cumnock when the Prince visited in 2001. As the website of The King's Foundation describes, it was considered 'a no-go zone ... torn apart by decades of harrowing violence'. Houses had been demolished or abandoned, the library and town hall were derelict. 'Piles of rubble, graffiti-strewn scrap metal and rubbish seemed at odds with its tropical assets: crystal-clear skies, Blue Mahoe trees and endless sunshine.' Four years later, the Prince's Foundation formed a plan with the local community to bring Rose Town back to life. Young people were trained in the crafts, the library was restored, barricades removed, and a women's enterprise project established in an apparently landmark Art Deco building (actually designed by Hugh Petter), along with a communal farm. The installation of ten standpipes brought running water back to the neighbourhood.

Rose Town is one of many initiatives that form an unarguable part of Charles's architectural legacy. Other aspects are less tangible. While his 'carbuncle' speech led to the replacement of a miserably procured design for the National Gallery with a more sympathetic, better funded successor, it also altered the public discourse about architecture for a generation. Senior figures in the profession could no longer say, in the words of Owen Luder, President of the RIBA, 'sod you' to the public. With the Prince's Paternoster Square intervention, Classicism climbed out of the small box in which it had been previously confined. There has been no general triumph for the style, which is still a minority taste; but it is practised with confidence by a growing number of architects and has become accepted as a valid way to work, particularly in association with historic buildings. Accusations of pastiche are heard less often. Looking back, it may have been that Charles was too doctrinaire: his root-and-branch opposition to Modernism in any form detracted from his big ideas about planning. Poundbury is big enough to absorb a few Modern buildings without detriment. Had it done so, it might have drawn the sting of some criticism. Style got the better of substance. But then, there was a war on. The Modernists were as bullying and authoritarian as some protagonists of the Culture Wars are today. To stand up to them took guts.

Other traditional methods of design and building are now standard. More respect is paid to old buildings. Through numerous initiatives Charles has also equipped a new generation of craftspeople and architects to add to the sum of happiness across Britain by creating beautiful structures, while gaining pleasure and satisfaction from their own working lives in the process.

Charles has not always been successful in his campaigns. He would have loved London to have a skyline akin to Venice, the one Sir Christopher Wren would have known when he built St Paul's, or that William Morris imagined in *News from Nowhere*. Instead it has been trashed by the proliferation of vulgar towers allowed by successive Mayors of London. Tall buildings have got taller. In 1984 the tallest building in Britain was Tower 42, better known as the NatWest Tower, designed by the most successful City architect of his generation, Colonel 'Richard' (in fact Reubin) Seifert, a pipe-smoking, Rolls-Royce-chauffeured operator, able to squeeze the maximum floor area out of any given site to boost rents. Little joy was to be had from these sub-Le Corbusian structures, wind tunnels at ground level and uncomfortable within. (Believe me on this: I worked in one for years.) The NatWest Tower was 183 metres tall. Today, Britain's tallest building – The Shard, designed by Renzo Piano – is 310 metres tall. People may argue over its merits but by any measure – imagination, technical performance, quality of materials – it is better than Tower 42. As Seifert's use of his military title indicates, his generation were still living under the shadow of the Second World War: there was little money or aspiration for architecture. Relatively speaking, Britain is now a land of plenty which can afford a better standard of construction as well as international architects like Piano. But then, The Shard is an exceptional building, – a one-off and not a blueprint for urban development. This is all too apparent in areas like Nine Elms Lane. The towers there, like most of high rises around London, are architectural dross.

The King should not, however, lose heart. Other aspects of contemporary architecture are less alien to his vision. For example, I was surprised to discover, when asked to help judge an architectural award, for an organisation whose President is the wizard of hi-tech Lord Foster, how many buildings on the shortlist made an impact through crafts such as bricklaying. They were good neighbours to the old buildings around them. Borough Yards, in Southwark, adjacent to some railway arches, is a salient example: this snaking, linear development, faced in brick, includes a section of restored arches to dramatic effect. One (the new restaurant at the former Chelsea Barracks) was even, in an astylar and stripped-down way, Classical. Would the world have taken this turn without Prince Charles's intervention in the architectural debate all those years ago? I would suggest not. To be sure, Modernism was also part of the shortlist's eclectic mix, represented by Nicholas Grimshaw's Battersea Power Station Underground Station. But we are now in an era of happy eclecticism. Let a hundred flowers bloom. Charles may not be keen on all the flowers but then not everybody likes his.

MacRobert
Farming & Rural Skills Cen
Opened by
H. M. King Charles III
on
16th September 2023

Charles has not only freed the human spirit by helping to make alternative approaches to architecture possible, giving heart to architects who practice in Classical or traditional styles, but he has been responsible for numerous educational initiatives to train young people. Here he is seen opening a centre for the study of farming and rural skills at Dumfries House in 2023.

Hurrah! The old hegemony has been broken. Charles can certainly take some of the credit for that. Indeed, it is the greatest part of his legacy: having made alternatives possible. He freed the human spirit, by opening the way to different creative approaches from those that had been previously available. Ben Bolgar's story can stand for others. Bolgar now occupies the position of executive director for projects at the King's Foundation, a reflection – should we be surprised? – of his rebelliousness as a student at Edinburgh College of Art in the 1980s. There he reacted against the unvaried diet of Modernism that his teachers were serving him. The latter could not understand his desire to follow a different path and they were not going to help him find his way.

> I tried to do a couple of traditional projects but was told to stop. Year 3 had a project at Charlotte Square, which is completely Georgian and so I decided to do a Georgian building. The School told me that if I was going to do classical architecture, I was on my own. Eventually I was asked to leave.

Through his summer schools, the Prince of Wales's Institute of Architecture and the Royal Drawing School, Charles opened a new avenue to hundreds of young people like Bolgar who were alienated from conventional art and architecture schools. As it happens, Bolgar has spent most of his working life in the orbit of the Prince. Other former students have taken different paths – and architectural education is itself changing. In this way it can be said that Charles has touched the lives of hundreds if not thousands of people, enabling them to follow their own line. He has not prescribed what that line should be. He has just made it possible to happen.

As Charles once said, he did not have to do this. He could have spent his Prince of Wales years playing polo. Instead he made himself vulnerable to criticism by laying his cards on the table and saying: These are the things I believe and these are the things that I like. He did not have to do it – but thank goodness he did. There have been moments of controversy and discord but for the most part we can call the result Harmony in practice. For this real and substantial achievement I warmly say: God save the King.

Appendix

Towns and cities in which the Urban Task Force was active, 1994–8.

Town/city (client or host)	Region	Date of involvement	Aim
Chinon (the mayor)	Loire, France	1994	Working on guidelines for an urban design unit within the city council.
Viterbo (the mayor and university)	Lazio, Italy	1994, 1995, 1998	Establishing a planning framework for the 50 acre site surrounding the convent-cum-prison of Santa Maria in Gradi
Caprarola (the mayor)	Lazio, Italy	1995	Preparing a scheme of renewal for five public squares, and making suggestions for the upgrading of a neighbouring suburb.
Biarritz (the mayor)	Pays Basque, France	1995	Preparing a plan for a cultural quarter.
St Petersburg (with the Repin Institute)	Russia	1996	The redesign of a theatre square.

Town/city (client or host)	Region	Date of involvement	Aim
Potsdam/Bornstedt (at the invitation of the Stadtbau-direktor)	Brandenburg, Germany	1996	Making a proposal for restituting the central square of the city, and suggestions for the extension of a historic village.
Berlin (at the invitation of the Senat)	Germany	1997	Formulating a proposal for the central Schlossplatz.
Beirut (with the private reconstruction company Solidere)	Lebanon	1997	Making sketch proposals for ways of joining the new central district to outlying areas.
Sidon (under the patronage of the Lebanese prime minister)	Lebanon	1997	Formulating a reconstruction plan for the Zouitini quarter.

From Brian Hanson and Samir Younés, 'Reuniting Urban Form and Urban Process: The Prince of Wales's Urban Design Task Force', *Journal of Urban Design*, vol. 6, no. 2 (2001), pp. 185–209.

Endnotes

EPIGRAPH

1 The letter was sold at auction in 2017.

1. CARBUNCLE

1 Alan Powers, 'David Watkin obituary', *The Guardian*, September 21, 2018.

2 Charles Saumarez Smith, *The National Gallery: A Short History*, (Frances Lincoln Limited Publishers, 2009), p. 156.

2. PEOPLE

1 When I interviewed him for a newspaper in 1988, it was in the converted farmhouse where he and his family had been living for ten years after exchanging the urban deprivation of Black Road for the solitude of the moors; as well as architectural salvage such as a wooden pulpit, it contained secret passages entered by tiny doors so that the Hackneys' young son could navigate the house unseen. Since he owned a construction firm as well as his architectural practice, the 'Hackney Empire', as my piece was headlined, had 300 projects underway across Britain. We don't need to feel too sorry for him.

3. CLASSICISM

1 Alan Hamilton, *The Real Charles*, (Collins, 1988), pp. 105–6.

2 Howell Raines, 'Defying Tradition: Prince Charles Recasts His Role', *New York Times*, February 21, 1988.

4. HARMONY

1 Robert J. Gordon, review of J.D.F. Jones, *Storyteller: The Many Lives of Laurens Van der Post*, *African Affairs*, vol. 101, no. 403 (April, 2002), pp. 270–71.

2 His Royal Highness The Prince of Wales, *Speeches and Articles 1968–2012*, ed. David Cadman and Sheila Bushrui (University of Wales Press, 2014), p. 1.

3 Theo Hobson, 'The Esoteric Creed of King Charles', *The Spectator*, September 17, 2022.

4 Mark Hoare, *A Painting Pilgrim: A Journey to Santiago de Compostela*, (Mudwall, 2003).

5 *pers. comm.* Brian Hanson.

6. ARCADIA

1 Isabel and Julian Bannerman, *Landscape of Dreams: The Gardens of Isabel and Julian Bannerman*, (Pimpernel Press Limited, 2016), p. 17.

2 Ibid., p. 16.

3 Roy Strong, *Types and Shadows: The Roy Strong Diaries, 2004–2015*, (Orion Publishing Group, 2020), p. 155.

7. UTOPIA

1 Kamal Ahmed and Vanessa Thorpe, 'Prince's pet village gets seal of approval', *The Observer*, May 14, 2000.

Picture Credits

Front cover: © Estate of Mark Boxer
Endpapers: © Drawing: Léon Krier / Watercolor: Ed Venn
15: © John Simpson Architects Ltd / Painting: Carl Laubin
19: Chronicle / Alamy Stock Photo
21: © Featherbottom & Partners
24: Richard Young / Shutterstock
31: RIBA Collections
36 top: Pjr Travel / Alamy Stock Photo
36 bottom: Andrew Holt / Alamy Stock Photo
42: © The Piper Estate / DACS 2024. Photo: Bridgeman Images
48: Trinity Mirror / Mirrorpix / Alamy Stock Photo
52: Homer Sykes / Alamy Stock Photo
54: Tim Graham / Getty Images
56: Mike Forster / Daily Mail / Shutterstock
64-65: © John Simpson Architects Ltd / Painting: Carl Laubin
69: Architectural Press Archive / RIBA Collections
71: Louis Hellman / RIBA Collections
83: © John Goodall / Country Life / Future Publishing Ltd
88: © Steven Brooke Studios
93: PA Images / Alamy Stock Photo
94: The Times / News Licensing
97: © Richard Ivey
101: PA Images / Alamy Stock Photo
110: Stephen Dorey - Bygone Images / Alamy Stock Photo
112: Les Wilson / Shutterstock

115: GAP Photos / Highgrove Gardens - Robert Smith
118: © Val Corbett / Country Life / Future Publishing Ltd
121: © Highgrove Gardens / Photographer: Niel Van Gijn
126-127: GAP Photos / Highgrove Gardens - A. Butler
134: GAP Photos / Highgrove Gardens - A. Butler
136: GAP Photos / Highgrove Gardens - A. Butler
138: GAP Photos / Highgrove Gardens - A. Butler
143: HTA Design LLP
152-153: iStock.com / Blackbeck
155: © Ben Pentreath
162: © Ben Pentreath
169: © Alireza Sagharchi / Photographer: Alex Boghian
170: © Alireza Sagharchi / Photographer: Alex Boghian
172: © Serban Bonciocat / www.transylvaniancastle.com
176: © Alireza Sagharchi / Photographer: Alex Boghian
177: © Alireza Sagharchi / Photographer: Alex Boghian
185: Findlay / Alamy Stock Photo
187 top: The Kings Foundation
187 bottom: The Kings Foundation
192: © Paul Barker / Country Life / Future Publishing Ltd
193: © Val Corbett / Country Life / Future Publishing Ltd
197 top: © Dylan Thomas / ADAM Architecture
197 bottom: © Hugh Hastings / ADAM Architecture
200: © Dylan Thomas / ADAM Architecture
204: © Hugh Hastings / ADAM Architecture
216-217: PA Images / Alamy Stock Photo

Every reasonable effort has been made to credit and acknowledge the ownership of copyright for illustrations, photography and artwork included in this book. Any errors that may have occurred are inadvertent and will be corrected in subsequent editions, provided notification is sent in writing to the publisher.

Index

Further Praise for the Triglyph People Series

SIR EDWIN LUTYENS:
BRITAIN'S GREATEST ARCHITECT?

'As someone who absolutely adores Lutyens and his work I didn't believe there was anything more I could discover about him … then this beautiful book comes along.' **George Clarke, Architect**

'Lively and scholarly, Aslet's concise biography, elegantly argues for Lutyens's place at the top table of British architecture.'
Loyd Grossman, Broadcaster and author

'Clive writes with effortless knowledge, bringing the trials and triumphs of Lutyens to life in a way that feels exciting and new.'
Ben Pentreath, House & Garden July 2024

'There are compelling reasons to revisit Lutyens, and nobody could do it better than Clive Aslet.'
Alan Powers, Country Life May 15, 2024

'*At the opening of this immaculate book, Clive Aslet, one of our most distinguished architectural historians, notes that there have been substantial biographies of Sir Edwin Lutyens, and he does not pretend to emulate them. His achievement, however, is considerable.*'

Simon Heffer, The Spectator May 18, 2024

'*Books can be polemic, books can be challenging, and sometimes books can just tell a good story. Clive Aslet's short biography of Lutyens tells a very good story – not entirely unknown but still packed with enough surprises to keep one reading to the very end.*'

Dr Stephen Games, Booklaunch Issue 20, July 2024

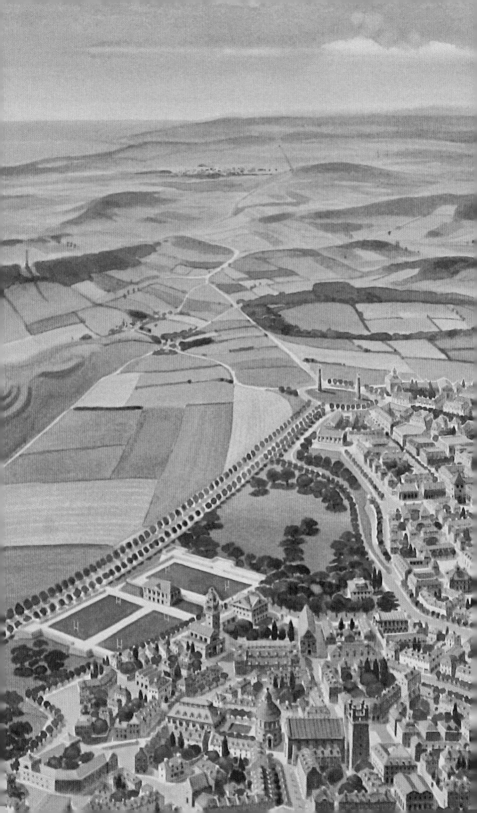